Some Leftover Verse

By Tom Matkin

Dedicated to
Betty, Patty, David, Katie, Amy, Ginger and Mark
and all the other wonderful family
they have brought into my life.

What's Inside

Page	Title
10	In Deepening Snow
11	Versifying
11	Home Teachers
12	The Grief of Missing
13	On the Altar
13	Lim'ricks and haiku
14	I Love the Sea
14	Making Career Choices
16	The Good and Bad of Parenting
16	Golfing With Jack
18	The Franklin Planner Blues
21	I Witness
21	You Know My Look
22	Stephen Crane v. Nathaniel Hawthorne
23	The Willow Tree
24	My Mule
26	In the Summer of 1960
28	I Am Reminded
29	My Treasures
31	Visiting the Lodge
32	The Boy
35	Misery
35	I Love the Man
36	Moonbeam
37	Step Into My Heart
41	Waiting
41	A Poem in the Wind
42	I Choose the Fall
43	The Master Mind
44	First Breath

45	*Christmas Shopping at Wal-Mart*
45	*Every Day*
46	*She Was a Woman*
47	*The Apostate Cat*
48	*Shaped By the Source*
49	*The Stroke*
49	*The Lost is Found*
50	*Grief is Underrated - Overlooked*
50	*A Pioneer Summary*
51	*Weeds and Seeds*
52	*Canto One*
53	*Canto Two*
53	*Canto Three*
54	*How Does it Feel?*
54	*Coralee and Katie*
55	*Flint in the Grass*
56	*The Serpentine Vine*
57	*Hurray for Wednesday*
57	*Workin' Yer Plate*
58	*That Cat*
59	*The Grizzly Blessing*
60	*The Boolean Blues*
61	*Out of the Grove*
62	*Try to Remember*
62	*A Part of Me Has Gone Ahead*
63	*Fear of Falling*
64	*If I was in the Olympics*
65	*Savage Digging*
66	*Haiku*
67	*Temptation*
68	*Sea of Glass*
69	*Review of "Dancing in the Wind"*
73	*Prolonging*

74	My Cheesy Thanksgiving Poem
75	I Shot a Bird
76	A Picture at an Old Soldier's Funeral
77	The Bow
77	In Solitary Wonder
78	Malchus (Luke 22:50-51)
78	Where Are You Going?
80	I Hear a Prophet
80	Hats
81	I See a Cloud
82	My List
82	Line Upon Line
83	The Moon
84	Maternal Blindness or Insight?
84	A Love Poem
85	Where is My Faith?
85	Quel Demise?
86	Yeah Sure
86	This March
87	Where Are You Going?
87	Asbestos I Can
88	Reflections on Alma 5
88	Cry for Love
89	Of Course
90	Walking
91	Some (Reflections on Helaman 13:38)
91	Things I Know
92	Tempered
92	Into the Wind
93	Shadows
93	I Went Gathering
94	Windy Doggerel
96	A Child's Poem

95	*Tender Mercies*
97	*So Average*
97	*Don't Bug Me*
98	*Reflections on Hebrews Chapter One*
99	*No Sonnet Today*
99	*Knot Like This*
100	*Redneck Love Poem – I think*
100	*Words That Rhyme with Smash*
101	*This Ragged Day*
101	*Sore Slack? Sit Back!*
102	*What's This*
102	*Green*
103	*Brushing*
104	*Temple Hymn*
105	*The Wind and Me*
105	*When the Church Burned Down*
106	*Lehi's Blues*
107	*Be Satisfied*
108	*The Blues*
108	*Shopping Mall Lights*
109	*Against the Greatest Certainty*
109	*Lettuce Sing the Blues*
110	*So Refreshing*
111	*Joe's Pigs*
118	*The Angel*
119	*The Gladiator*
120	*How is the War Going?*
121	*Sweeping Up*
122	*My Life*
123	*The Race*
124	*Reflections on Barbara Olsen 1955-2001*
125	*The Flag and the Duster*

127	Hack in the Hack
128	The Horseshoe
129	Jacob & Ezra (Reflections on Pride)
130	Club President
130	My Pledge (A Song of Sartorial Suffering)
132	Ties – A Rant
133	Your Eyes
133	the devil's mirror
134	I Like to Eat it All
135	This Easter Morn
135	Breaking Bread
136	Approaching the Harbour of New Orleans (1853)
136	Approaching Saint Louis (1853)
137	Approaching the Valley (1853)
137	A News Haiku
138	How Ya Gonna Go?
139	My Gripe With Harper Lee
140	Salmon on Toast
140	Quecreek Mine
141	Speed Skating
140	In a Parallel Universe
142	You Could Feel the Winter Wind
142	The Book of Mormon (My Complaint)
143	In This Bumpity Bumpity Truck that we Ride
144	Be a Lawyer
144	I Ask Myself a Question
146	The Starting Line
147	Rolling Coins
148	How Do You Like Your Eggs?
149	Perhaps You've Heard …
150	November Wind
151	Cheering them on
152	I See You

153	*I Sleep on Live Coals*
153	*Summer Morning*
154	*Visiting Liberty*
155	*Got it Done*
156	*Saturday's Work*
156	*This Riddle*
157	*The Winter After He Died*
158	*This fumbling testing time*
159	*Into the School of Plenty*
160	*After Seminary Grad*
160	*Picture on the Funeral Home Wall*
161	*Why You Can't Go Home Again*
166	*Reflections on D&C 18:10*
166	*My Hands*
167	*Shopping at Costco*
168	*Riding Above the River*
168	*What Rhymes with Blood?*
169	*Too Tired to Count*
170	*When You Joined This Church*

In Deepening Snow

In deepening snow these two met.
Which saw the other first
They could not know,
And of the
Meeting
Each
Was equally glad.
She had fallen deep asleep.
And he not understanding,
And little remembering
Left the house
To seek
Help
When he
Could not awake her.
Fearful and confused he ran
Through the snow
And deep into
The night.
Meanwhile she
Awoke and felt his absence.
At the very moment she was noticing
That his shoes were still
Sitting neatly by
The door,
He was
Breathlessly sobbing out his fear
To their son.
Who followed quickly
Back towards their
House and arrived
Just as they
Met in the
Snow.

Versicising

Some will sharpen their wits
On the daily crossword puzzle.
And others play at games like chess
To keep their minds from fuzzle.

Cause it's important to exercise
And stretch our capacities mental
As we get old and suffer hardening
Of arteries like metal

So I suggest a dandy way
To help old Noggin well.
Each day write a dozen lines
Of simple rhyming doggerel.

Home Teachers

I'm sad when my Home Teachers
Leave their visit to the last,
And come to me at time of month

When most the days have past.

It sort of makes me wonder
Do they really care for me?
Or are they only coming
To say they've done their duty?

It makes me feel I'm second rate
And that I've been forgotten
And truth be told I whine a bit
And hint to them, they're rotten.

But there's one thing 'bout comin' late
That bothers me each time.
If I must stay and meet with THEM
When can I go do mine?

The Grief of Missing

The grief of missing
The brass ring
As it swings
So very
Close
Is
Known
To us all.
We watch it swing
Within our
Grasp
And
In
An
Instant
It will fly away....
Much further than ever before.
But as we study times
When magically
The ring
Was
In
Our
Hand to stay!
We must admit that many times
The happier
Chance
Was
In
Missing.

On the Altar

On the altar, wrapped in cloth
(And when he had given thanks,)
Prepared in solemn form
(he brake it, and said, Take, eat:)
Are the body and the blood.
(this is my body, which is broken for you:)
Blood poured out and body torn
(this do in remembrance of me.)
As sacred hymns are sung.
(After the same manner also he took the cup,)
Then kneeling. Just a child really,
(when he had supped, saying,)
Will offer prayer on my behalf
(This cup is the new testament in my blood)
Asking to remember sincerely
(this do ye, as oft as ye drink it, in remembrance of me.)
The living water and bread of life
(For as often as ye eat this bread,)
That now is shrouded in the pall.
(and drink this cup,)
Blessing as I eat and drink it
(ye do shew the Lord's death)
That I'll covenant to give my all.
(till he come.)

Lim'ricks and haiku

Lim'ricks and haiku
Not so much poems as leaves
Of thought in the breeze.

I Love the Sea

Deep as the sea is my love of it.
Walking its shores.
Plumbing its depths.
Riding its shoulders.
Sensing its peace and
Feeling its rage.
Hearing its heartbeat.
Looking across its broad back into the sky.
Where it connects with a shining line.
Whether in rough weather,
With powerful wave,
And terrible tide, secretive foam,
And lashing, crashing, dashing, splashing spray;
Or in the calm,
Watching shimmering ribbons of moon light
Dancing into me from heaven,
I love the sea.

Making Career Choices

I think all honest jobs are fine
Though some may leave me flat.
I'd never want to have to ask,
"Would you like fries with that?"

And working hard in outdoor air
May clear your lungs and skin up
But I find muscles weak as mine
Can't even do a chin up.

And some careers require a touch
Of people person skills.
Though what I call diplomacy
Others call a test of wills.

And then there's work that takes real brains
The rocket science stuff.
I thought of doing some of that...
But thinking was enough.

And teaching others takes a gift
Of confidence and poise
That never quite appealed to me
It makes less sense than noise.

And what about the animals?
Someone must care for our pets!
You mean those messy smelly things?
I'll leave all that to vets.

Or fixing things that wear or break
Is tidy honest toil
But one thing stops me doing that...
My allergy to oil.

I might have been a lot of things
That working hard produces
But 'stead of doing all of that
I just produce excuses!

The Good and Bad of Parenting

The good and bad of parenting
Is shown in this common thing
Most modern beds are "Queen" or "King"
And much more comfort seem to bring
So kids will often climb in bed
□Tween mom and dad and this is said,
The kid may snuggle, kiss and love ya,
Or push and kick and really shove ya.
And most your pillow will want to share
But that can mean feet in your hair.
And steal you blankets, but here's the charm
Other kids will cuddle up and keep you warm.
While others sweat and heat like pokers,
Still others are cold, they're frosty jokers.
Yes some will stroke and gently treat you,
While others flail and cruelly beat you.
And ride and rake you with their spurs
Until by morning you□re ready for nurse.
Yes all this is nuisance or great fun
But more important when all is done
There is one thing strong as breath,
One thing that comes as sure as death.
Sometime that child will feel not right
And get sick on you in dead of night.

Golfing With Jack

I was golfing all night with Jack Nicholas
He was favouring his hip quite a lot
His short game was fine and his putting was good
But his driving was certainly not.

It was sad in a way to see it from near
You can live with it when it's afar

But the man is unhappy to struggle like that
He's accustomed to being a star.

So I tried to cheer him and help him
I told him he wasn't so bad
But he seemed to resent whatever I said
My words were just making him mad.

I let him drive from the easier tees
And I offered to spot him some strokes
But I still could easily beat him
And he snarled a bit at my jokes.

I told him that when it came morning
I'd bother him then, not at all
But for now he was mine to be sure
And I confidently teed up my ball.

My waggle was best of all waggles
I struck it with power and skill
My follow through was a pure classic
And the ball flew high over the hill.

When Jack saw I had hit such a wonder
He braced and resolved to do best
But his hip let him down and he slipped
And topped that ball just like the rest.

Oh I tried to comfort and please him
I offered him all sorts of advice
I tried to improve and to cheer him
By telling him his game was still "nice".

Yes I love to go golfing at night time
It beats what I do in the day
Yeah, I golfed all last night with Jack Nicholas
And next time, with a Tiger I'll play.

The Franklin Planner Blues

Okay, here is the gig. I will take the harp solos and play the rhythm guitar. You there, with the vacant look in your eye. You play the drums.

And you, with that look that kills, you play the bass guitar, and young man. Yes, you with the innocent look and the long hair and nose ring.

Yes you. You take this Van Halen special and play the lead licks. Okay now. Who will sing?

Let's divide that up. Anyone in the place with a Franklin planner? I know this is a Stake High Priests Social and that most of you didn't think you would need your planners, but who has one? Okay, then President Smith, Bishop Olsen, Brother Laverock and Brother Paxman. Come up here and stand in line behind the microphone. You will each do a verse of the song. Try to remember not to sing Bishop Olsen. I'm not worried about the rest of you, I've heard you try to sing before and I know it won't happen. Just read your lines. The band will make it musical.

Okay now in lieu of a rehearsal let me explain how this will go. The designated blues shouter will read a line then the band will do the classic blues vamp. You know that Pillsbury dough thing "duh DUH duh DUH". Then the shouter will deliver the next line and so forth until he reaches the end of the verse. Then we will take a 12 bar blues musical break. Lead guitar will take the first solo, I'll go after the second verse with my blues harp, (Aside to the lead guitar man) Can you play rhythm while I do my harp thing? You do know what chords are don't you? Well just fake it then. We'll be in "A"so just start near the middle of the neck of the guitar. After the next verse we will go back to the guitar solo and lets just throw all we've go into the final riff. Actually. Lets do 2 or 3 sets of 12 bars at the end. I'll let you know when we've milked it enough. Got it? Here we go.

President Smith:
You wake up in the morning and roll over in bed trying to remember just who and where you are;
"duh DUH duh DUH"
You can☐t even remember your name or   anything about yourself, or how to find out;
"duh DUH duh DUH"
Suddenly your arm reaches out instinctively and your hand grabs a hold of your external brain;
"duh DUH duh DUH"
You pop open your Planner and turn to the tab marked TODAY and there you are and
everything about you;
"duh DUH duh DUH"
YOU'VE GOT THE FRANKLIN PLANNER BLUES
(12 BAR BLUES LICK - LEAD GUITAR SOLO)
Bishop Olsen:
You just got a Church call and you have a hopeless tangle of meetings, agendas,
interviews, training sessions and ppi's;
"duh DUH duh DUH"
You can't sleep at night, you can't relax by day, and your evenings are full of a whirl of people and problems;
"duh DUH duh DUH"
It's fear of forgetting that paralyzes your mind, so you carry this book wherever you go;
"duh DUH duh DUH"
A Franklin Planner is grafted permanently to your hand, you have no excuse for missing anything or anybody;
"duh DUH duh DUH"
Oh Yeah, you have no excuse for missing anything or anybody;
"duh DUH duh DUH"
YOU'VE GOT THE FRANKLIN PLANNER BLUES

(12 BAR BLUES MUSICAL BREAK - HARP SOLO)
Brother Laverock:
You know all about completing "Daily Record of Events",
you never fail to fill out a "Master Task List"
"duh DUH duh DUH"
You have your values and goals written carefully in the
proper spot and you
constantly refer to your "Prioritized Daily Task List";
"duh DUH duh DUH"
The day consists of "Tasks completed", "Tasks Planned
Forward", "Tasks Deleted", "Delegated Tasks" and "Tasks in
Process";
"duh DUH duh DUH"
Your life is fulfilling and perfectly prioritized, you know
what is urgent or merely desirable;
"duh DUH duh DUH"
YOU'VE GOT THE FRANKLIN PLANNER BLUES
(12 BAR BLUES MUSICAL BREAK - LEAD GUITAR
SPOTLIGHT)
Brother Paxman:
So your call is simple, you never miss an assignment, your
every minute is planned, It's heaven on earth.
"duh DUH duh DUH"
But amidst all this bliss is a nagging concern, a feeling of
loss and doubt that won't go away;
"duh DUH duh DUH"
The question that gets you is what would you do without it?
What COULD you do without it?
"duh DUH duh DUH"
Your real brain is useless and your memory is shot, a book
has replaced your SOUL;
"duh DUH duh DUH"
YOU'VE GOT THE FRANKLIN PLANNER BLUES
(12 BAR BLUES LICKS UNTIL THE BAND TIRES OUT)

I Witness

These people are all strangers to me,
Except the Sealer who has invited me to witness
This woman, this 60 year old woman,
This beautiful woman, this beautiful stranger
Kneel between her very pregnant daughter
And that daughter's strong and worthy husband
At the altar
While the Sealer pronounces great blessings
Upon this woman,
Joining her, at last, at long last, to her parents
As we each weep and
I witness.

You Know My Look

You know my look.
Sackcloth on my back,
ashes on my head,
foot in my mouth,
nose to the grindstone,
ear to the ground,
elbows to the grease,
feet in the clouds,
hands in the air,
thumbs up,
heart on the sleeve,
chin up,
chest out,
stomach in,
tongue out,
eyes crossed
and hair lost.

Stephen Crane v. Nathaniel Hawthorne

Announcer: Could I have your attention pullleease! In this corner we have a callow youth. A soldier I'd guess. Wearing a red badge of courage. And in his corner, his trainer, Stephen Crane.   And in the opposite corner Hester Prynne, wearing a .... a.... scarlet letter! And trained by Nathaniel Hawthorne. Just a
minute here. Judges, how is this going to work, they're both in red? Won't there be confusion.

Chief Judge: Confusion. Confusion. Of course there'll be confusion. Generations of high school literature students will be trying to sort this fight out for centuries. Let's get on with it.

Announcer: Now this will be a 10 round fight and the winner.... Hey, just a minute, you there, youth from the red corner, where are you goin'? I say, come back here, there is supposed to be a fight! Crane, won't you get your man back here to fight?

Crane: I shall do my best sir to see that the pride of these games is maintained.

Hester: (Calling to the retreating youth) Shall we not meet again?

Hawthorne: Hester, it's farewell.

The Crowd: (various shouts) What's happening? No fight tonight? I don't understand!

The Willow Tree

This willow tree of mine came from hardy stock.

I cut a young and healthy branch off the willow
That grew at my father's place, below the spring
On a sunny southern slope and whose trunk was
Wide and strong and supported long and thick
Limbs which held swing ropes and daring young
Climbers and whose broad shade protected us at
Lunch or during a nap on a hot day.

My start was eight feet long and I planted it four
And poured the water to it, and it made a quick try
To blossom and shoot into the air, but exhausted
By a lack of roots it fell back and for years would
Only cling to life.

Early one winter, after a dry and cold fall I gave up
On the young willow and decided to pull it up,
But it would not yield and not finding my ax
I left it for another spring.

And when the season changed and my heart too
I saw in brave new shoots and courageous leaves
That there was still promise, and life, and hope
In the young willow and so I offered more water,
Trimmed back the dead parts and watched.

And this year, only this year, after so many,
The young willow is reaching now to heaven
With high and outstretched arms, and it bows
Gracefully with the wind and shocks my eyes
With bright and lovely leaves and shiny bark,
Offering real shade and the promise soon of a place
For another child's swing, it's roots now deep
Beneath my garden.

My Mule

A fella once told me his mule
Could the work of two horses do
And didn't ever need, very much feed
And made a swell partner too.

And he said how his mule wouldn't wander
Or ever get sick or sore feet
And he gave me the line, that the mule was just fine
For ploughing in cold or in heat

And so I agreed to buy me that mule
And I'm happy as punch to report
That most what he told, was as good as gold
Just as true as an oath in a court.

But when it came time to go ploughin'
There came to my honest attention,
I'm sure you will find, it just slipped his mind,
Some things he'd forgotten to mention

The first thing was really a trifle
T'wernt hardly worth saying a word
But it might help you care, and be more aware
So it's better if it's something you've heard.

I noticed that when I was harnessing my pet
That the kick of the animal was strong
And his heels caught me square, and carried me. Where?
On an trip that turned out to be long.

It took bout a week to find my way back
His kick was much more than a tap
So I learnt not to find myself near his behind,
Unless carryin compass and map.

The other problem I had was more
grave
I just couldn't get that mule to go.
He was harnessed I saw, and I shouted "HEE HAW"
But he just stood there and looked at me so.

I tackled the problem with noise and with force
I used whips, sticks and switches with all of my might
I pulled on a rope, and I pushed on that dope
And I shook him with dynamite.

I rolled him on logs and pulled on his ears
And I dangled some carrots in front of his nose
I spit in his eyes, and slid him on ice
And enlisted the help of wild wolves

I carried on trying such a lot of good things
Without any mule movement at all
And after a year, I was beginning to fear
That this critter would be my downfall

When just in the nick of time I met
The man who had sold me that mule
And I asked him to show, how to make that mule go
And I hoped he could save this poor fool

Then he slapped at his forehead and said he was sorry
And my problem he hoped he could ease.
"I musta forgot," he said, after thought
"That mule never moves. Unless you say 'Please'."

In the Summer of 1960

In the summer of 1960
I was 11 and for the 5th summer in a row,
I was living in Missoula, Montana.
I was playing baseball on
Everyday but Sunday
And watched a satellite
Cross the night sky for the first time
In my life
While a home run went unnoticed to
End an extra inning game for the Timberjacks.
And I perched on the score board
In center field and hung the numbers
While the American Legion teams played and
After, I ran the bases and stood on the mound
Where those, on the way up, and those,
Down from the majors, played.
I met a boy who could throw a wonderful sweeping curve
ball
And he had a catcher's mitt and I begged him everyday
To let me catch his curve ball for as long as he would throw
it
And I was filled with inexplicable joy
Every time I saw it break.
And I played tennis while U.S. Air Force
Fighter jets flew low overhead
And I rode my bike in the evening with no hands
Across the quiet squares of
University of Montana, under cover of huge green trees,
Where my Father was a student.
And I caught butterflies and drank cold
A & W Root Beer for a nickle and
Warm Canada Dry Ginger Ale
Given to me by a kindly neighbour in our
Hot, small, wartime strip housing complex
With no airconditioning and no stove or oven

And picked huckleberries in the canyon
And never thought about not having a T.V..
And I lay on my back on the ground at night with
My ball glove for a pillow and watched the lightening
Rip across the sky, terrifying the hills they called
mountains
And freezing the night into a pale and shadowy day for an
instant.
I pitched for my team and we went to the city finals
Against a team from across town whose players
Were all black and
Where in the first inning
I hit a triple up against the fence,
And scored our only run
Before striking out three times and
Knowing, for the first time, that
I was too slow for the game,
And, on that same day,
Getting into our car and going,
Directly from the ball diamond,
Home to Canada and never coming back
Until I was married with children of my own,
Who showed little interest in where the
Ballpark used to be but
Enjoyed a visit to a mall that didn't use to be there.

I Am Reminded

On the highway to Calgary
Near a hamlet called Granum
Is an old and smallish country
Cemetery where lies
The remains of a young boy
Who died suddenly and tragically
When, as he hurried to his duty,
He tripped,
And fell on his pitch fork.

The headstone has a small
Stone carving of a pair of
Boys worn boots neatly
Placed together and covered
By a boy's woollen cap.

A silent reminder in death
Of a tidy obedient child in life.

Long since the boy's own boots
And woolen cap are gone
From his simple bedroom but
They stay locked in the
Hearts of those who mourn.

Come with me to Calgary
And we will stop for five minutes
Together along the way
And seek out this grave
And reverently brush back any weeds
That may have overgrown
And quietly we will study
That silent stone carving.
Then drive away with new
Stirrings in our hearts.

My Treasures

I'm staring at my precious things,
The things I really care about
Things stacked around my office
Things I'd never ever throw out.

I'm seeking as the Elf might ask
To see with my poet's eye
The true value of these objects d'art,
And I'm trying not to cry.

What stories these dear items
Could tell us if they spoke
What tragedies and hardships
Because most of them are broke.

I mean, it really cries of art
To see an Wingman Warrior joystick
Cast lovingly in a cardboard box
Reminding of a bygone war so sick.

And boxes full of floppy disks
The sizes no one uses
Foreshadow soft and hardware death
And stimulates my muses.

And on the wall a map or two
Each covered by those post-it notes
And calendars and phone lists
Symbolic. And also food for goats.

And on my shelf an old hard drive
Cast off for lack of megabytes
And modems too, not a few
That lost the baud speed fights.

And packages of sugar free gum
And sesame seed treats
That comfort me in late of night
When I feel the need for sweets.

Or on the floor a lot of boxes
That packaged different software
Some is new and some is old
But all are proof that life's unfair.

And files aplenty in my room
Abound and scatter round
Telling me that what is sure
Is if it's lost it must be found.

And as I look at power outlets
With cords from each in dozens
And phone lines running everywhere
And LAN lines that are cousins

I realize the network sweet
That makes the fabric of our lives
And connects me with my virtual pals
Buzzes just like so many bee hives.

Yes there's real meaning in the books
That I've stacked on bench and floor
And manuscripts and canceled checks
Gathered like thoughts on life's great shore.

So everyone, I've loved this task
Of looking well upon my stuff
And hope this glance at one percent
Of all my mess is quite enough.

Visiting the Lodge

The names are graven into plastic.
Solid names of solid people on flimsy plastic.
Each is temporary and easy to remove and replace.
The plan is obvious to all. These names will go one day.
Although some are yellowing, time and light affect plastic
that
way.

The doors are powered, automatic, sliding, quiet.
Double doors to catch the weather and keep it out.
Glass doors that filter light and reflect the inside out and
outside in.
Doors you never have to tug or lean on.
Doors that seem to understand.
Doors not locked til after hours, doors that never touch
your
outstretched hand.

Down a long and narrow hallway, carpet taking snow
from your
feet.
Doors and names on either side, find the one you want
today.
Remember as you read the names and force the senses
To hear and smell and feel and see and taste
Then stop and knock and wait.

Give a happy salutation to a solid someone on a plastic
plaque
Shout your business, and smile broadly
Shake hands carefully and quickly.
And patiently accept this fate,
Those doors for you await.

The Boy

There was just a hint of dawn
As the boy first began trudging
Down the narrow gravel road.
It would take him about 10 minutes,
At his normal sleepy pace,
To reach the place where the road ended.

By the time he got there the trees in the grove
At the end of the road were silhouetted
Against the glow of the rising sun.
The cows were pressed up to the gate
Almost bowling him over as he opened it.
They knew the routine and they marched
Back up the road the way he had come.
He left the gate down
So that when the milking was done
The cows could let themselves back into the pasture
And work their way down to the river
Where there was water, shade and lots of grass.

He didn't know what caught his attention first,
The noise or the movement,
But he turned quickly towards it.
High in the trees
Outlined against what was now a morning sky
Were two crows.
He stopped very still and watched them.
All of the cows were up the road forgotten.
Crows are smart. Wary.
And usually you can't get near them.
The boy had tried many times.
They seemed almost smarter than he was.
It was as if they watched him watching them
And then kept a measured distance away from him.
A distance that seemed to double if you held a rifle.

He had long ago decided
That to bag a crow would be an achievement.
But having decided to shoot one
And then actually getting the chance to do it,
Those were two different things.
And now these crows were just perched there in front of
him.
He couldn't believe his good fortune.

Snapping back to reality he broke into a quick trot,
Trying to watch his step in the poor light,
But checking back over his shoulder as often as he dared
To see if the crows were still there.
They were.
He caught the cows just before the yard gate
Made sure they turned into the milk house corral.
He had already put a bucket of chopped grain
In the feeding bin at the head of each stall
It was no trouble getting the first 8 cows into place,
He quickly slid the neck locks in place and began washing
the
udders.
The old man had cleaned and prepared the automatic
milkers
And was beginning to actually milk.
The boy was finished his part in their ritual
He knew that it would be 20 minutes
Before he would be expected to chase in the second batch.
Without a word he quickly he ran back to the house
Grabbed his .22 single shot from the closet on the porch.
He fumbled for a box of shells
And then ran for the end of the road.

It was daylight by the time he got there
He could clearly see,
As he neared the grove,
That the crows were still there.

33

They were noisy and agitated by his coming
But they didn't fly away.
He loaded quickly and took aim
At the one perched just above the nest.
It was only 30 yards away.
The first shot found the mark easily
The crow tumbled out of the tree,
Dead before it hit the ground.
He watched as the other crow went crazy,
Screaming and flying from branch to branch,
First moving to the nest then away.
Then it swooped down,
Right at him,
Filling him with fear.
But it was just a ruse,
The crow only pretended to attack
And then flew away,
Hopping madly through the high branches in the grove.
The boy loaded his gun again
And the first time the crow sat still for just an instant,
He shot it dead.
It fell not far from the other.

"Wow," he said aloud,
To no one but himself.
"I've finally killed a crow.
Two crows!"
He stood over the bodies
Marveled at how big they were.
And how black.
Then he shielded his eyes
Against a bright low risen sun
Looked up at the nest,
And for the first time he realized
Why the crows had not flown away.

Misery

Pain will come to one and all
But misery is optional.

Haiku Envy

And I wish that I could write haiku
Just the way that those Asians can do
So in season and sync
They show us how to think
And make much about nothing ado.

I Love the Man

I love the Man with all seeing eye,
Who moves the mountain
And paints the sky.

I love the Man who commands the wave
Who made the earth
And loves to save.

I love the Man who lights the stars
Who offers grace
And changes hearts.

I love the Man who makes birds sing.
Who is my Brother,
Savior, Friend and King.

I love Man who paints the sky
Who loves me too
And hears my cry!

Reflecting on the following statement:

"A testimony is fragile. It is as hard to hold as a moonbeam. It is something you have to recapture every day of your life." Harold B. Lee (Church News, July 15, 1972, page 4)

Moonbeam

The moonbeam's fragile ghostly glint
Graces somber blackened flint
With sparkling points of precious light
Which viewed alone take back the night

The moonbeam plays across a face
And passes there with happy trace
Its measured light just skips along
Exposing cracks 'tween right and wrong.

The moonbeam isn't found on days,
In clouds or mists or out of phase,
It brightens only when the sun
It's earthly work is o'er and done.

Oh seek that precious gift of light
And harbour it against the night
You need it not in heart of day
But when the sun will steal away.

Step Into My Heart

Elder Kenney was singing quietly. You would have described it as "singing under his breath". But he was singing. It was his song. He was from Wyoming and had grown up listening to country and western radio stations against his will, and as a final act of rebellion he had crafted his own awful parody of a country and western song. Which he sang almost constantly. And this song, which had been born of rebellion and disgust for a genre that he felt no part of, but which he could not escape, had become a part of him. You will not be surprised to learn that soon after returning to Wyoming, Elder Kenney would find that country and western music had changed enough to become more to his liking and that very soon after being home he would stop singing his song and soon after that he would forget all about it.

But for now he was singing it. Carrying out this constant protest against who he was and where he came from. A protest which had also become a constant reminder of a place that was home.

"Step into my heart,"

Elder Kenney knocked on a door. There was noise behind it but no one came to the door. He knocked again.

"Dear, dear, dear...."

They moved on to the next door in the long hallway. He peered through the dim light and tried to count how many doors there were on the floor of the apartment building. His companion was keeping the tracting book and Elder Kenney was enjoying the perk of rank, not having to pay attention to the details of their morning's harvest. When he had been a junior companion he actually had sort of

37

enjoyed the challenge of keeping a neat and accurate tracting book, but now he enjoyed not being bothered with it too.

"Step into my heart,"

They moved together to the next door. It was his companion's turn to knock. They always took turns. One door would be Elder Kenney's and the next would belong to his companion. If it was your door you knocked and you did the talking. If it wasn't your door you were free to think, or not think. Free to observe, or not. Or you could do subtle things to try to make your companion laugh during his door approach, or not.

But, of course, here in a big apartment building in the middle of the morning, in the middle of the week, no one would answer the doors anyway. So it didn't matter what you did. I didn't matter if it was your door or not.

"Dear, dear, dear,"

Sixteen, it looked like. Sixteen doors in that hallway. Eight on each side with stairways at either end. It was a 4 story walk up. They were on the third floor working their way down from the top. Probably every apartment was exactly like the other. The hall smelled of apartment building. That strange and indeterminate mix of garlic, sweat, cabbage, onions and urine. Always urine. Why couldn't the French learn to pee in the pot he wondered. In Wyoming people didn't urinate in the stairway of their own apartment buildings. At least he didn't think they did. He had never actually been in an apartment building in Wyoming.

"I love you,"

They finished knocking on all the doors on the third floor

and rattled quickly and noisily down the stairs to the
second floor. Elder Kenney may have been an old
missionary, but he was still a young man. And young men
make something of stairs. Whether climbing them or
descending they bring out the boy in the young man. Stairs
break the monotony. Take them two or three at a
time. Swing wildly around hand rails. Stumble noisily.
Don't even bother to stop to catch your breath when you
get to the next level. It comes back to you almost instantly,
always before a door can be answered.

Now for the big finish to his song. A full measure for each
word.

"So... step... in... my... heart."

His companion looked at him with a pained look. Looking
like he might want to step on Elder Kenney's heart himself.
They had only been together for 3 weeks, but this was quite
possibly the thousandth time he had heard the "big finish"
and it always reminded him that the noise that came from
Elder Kenney was actually a song. One time he had woke
up in the middle of the night. Had *been* awakened
actually. As he stilled his own breath and tried to figure
out what had woke him he heard Elder Kenney singing his
song. His companion should have been sleeping. Snoring or
just slow regular breathing in his bed across the room. But
instead. Elder Kenney, from Wyoming, was lying there at
4:00 a.m. in the darkness, singing.

"Step into my heart
Dear, dear, dear....
Step into my heart
Dear, dear, dear....
I love you,
So... step... in... my... heart."

It had troubled him. Was Elder Kenney singing in his sleep? Or was he actually awake at 4:00 a.m. and singing? Which was worse? As he tried to figure it out, and before he could actually summon the good sense to call out and ask, he had fallen back to sleep.

By the time they finished the apartment building it was almost noon. They went to the bus stop to wait for the city bus to pick them up and take them to the business district where they would buy lunch and run some personal errands before returning for a full afternoon of tracting. The complex they were tracting out had 41 buildings exactly like the one they had just finished and they were only about 1/3 complete. They could cover about 10 a day, unless someone invited them in.

"Step into my heart."

Elder Kenney was leaning against the bus shelter with his eyes closed. He picked up the tempo and the volume of his song.

"Dear, dear, dear.....
Step into my heart,"

The bus pulled up to the curb and the door swung open.

"I love you,"

His companion pushed into the cavern of the bus. Elder Kenney started, then turned to the empty street and flung out his arms. Big finish.

"So... step... in... my... heart."

Then he jumped into the bus and it bore them away.

40

Waiting

Tapping my foot,
Pretending to sleep.
Stretching my back
Counting some sheep.
Trying to read
Unable to think.
Chewing my gum
Getting a drink.
Checking my watch
Eyeing the crowd.
Not hearing music
Turned up too loud.
Cool as fire,
Patient as ice.
Feels like my head
Is stuck in a vice.
I'm waiting.

A Poem into the Wind

I sent a poem into the wind
It was tossed and wildly blown
And when the wind had stopped
I wondered where it had flown.

I sent a poem into the wind
It blew up against a fence
And held that place for days
But now has been driven hence.

I sent a poem into the wind
On a warm uplifting breeze
It soured high and far and wide
As effortlessly as you please.

I sent a poem into the wind
Which grabbed and wore and tore it
And fragments scattered everywhere
There was no way to store it.

I sent a poem into the wind
It was tossed and wildly blown
And when the wind had stopped
I wondered where it had flown.

I Choose the Fall

The winter poet's icy breath
Is charged with images of death.
The spring poet's lively scope
Reminds of love, new life, and hope.

The summer poet eyes the increase,
And warmth that brings us inner peace.
But the autumn poet's task is best
His joy and sorrow exceeds the rest.

In every fall the seeds for spring
Promise us what summer will bring.
In summer what will, will grow,
And by the fall, true worth will show.

And winter's shadow on us falls
When harvest ends with bitter squalls
So if such a thing can be from choice
I choose the fall for my poet's voice.

The Master Mind

The HUMan MIND is LOTS of FUN.
Its STRETCHes KNOW no END
It TWISTS and BENDS and CHEATS,
With EV'ry CHANGing TREND.

It SPREADS itSELF so VEry THIN
Or SWITches 'ROUND to THICK.
It GETS as SOFT as MUSH
Or SETS up LIKE a BRICK

The MIND can TRAP a COMplex FACT
And KEEP it FOR a QUIZ.
Or CAST aWAY the THOUGHT
Of WHERE your PARKED car IS.

It HELPS us KEEP a SLIGHT or GRUDGE
ReMEMB'ring JUST who DONE it
And MAGniFY the evil DEED
RePLACing PEACE with HAVoc.

But MOSTly IT will JUST forGET
UnLESS it's BEEN reMINDed
Of THINGS that REALly MATter
It SEEMS so EAS'ly BLINDed.

So I proPOSE we TAKE comMAND
And NEVer LEAVE the MIND
To WANder WHERE it WILL
Cause DANger IT might FIND.

And LEARN this TRUTH that SOME forGET,
Don't LET the MIND conTROL.
It ONly RENTS - not OWNS -
The LANDlord IS your SOUL.

BeCOME the MASter OF your MIND.
And MAKE this PLAStic FRIEND
More DISciPLINED and KIND,
AVOID a TRAgic END -
BeCOME the MASter OF your MIND.

First Breath

On
A sudden call
But not unexpected
I drove 12 hours yesterday to hold a baby
Not yet born when I started,
But born
By the
Time
I
Arrived
And as I held
Him his wonderful
Parents described their
Joy and wonder at his first
Breath and my Spirit
Was more alive
Today
As
I
Drove
Twelve more hours
To return to my home
And as I took notice anew
Of my own breath of life
And was filled with
Wonder.

Christmas Shopping at Wal-Mart

When people get together
They pass along diseases,
In crowds, in throngs, in mobs,
Like flus, and colds, and sneezes.
And Christmas time is the worst
At parties and programs and shows
We're thrown together with strangers
And germs are spread head to toes.
But just today I noticed
Sickness from a whole new page
Took hold of me at Wal-Mart...
A mild case of shopping cart rage.

Every Day

Your next door neighbour doesn't die every day.
The one who fed your kids candy and let them call her
"Grandma
Card"
Baked you apple pies
Greeted you in Church
Let your kids glean her raspberries bushes and play with
her
puppy.
And always asked about them after they grew up and
moved away.
Your next door neighbour for over 20 years and a friend
For 30 years before that.
No, someone as close as all that to you doesn't die every
day,
But she did die on Saturday.
And now you remember,
Somebody does die every day.

She Was a Woman

She was a wide woman
With a broad face
Lots of shoulders and a narrow waist
That blossomed out into big hips
Sturdy legs and solid feet.

She was a kind woman
With a soft gaze
Lots of patience and an easy laugh
That blossomed out into a great smile
Sturdy countenance and warm eyes.

She was a strong woman
With a sure heart
Lots of courage and confidence
That blossomed out into self assurance
Sturdy faith and honest trust.

She was a sad woman
With a deep hurt
Lots of pain and worry
That blossomed out into empathy
Sturdy friendship and true compassion.

She was a woman.

The Apostate Cat
by Tom Matkin

He prowls around
His Master's yard.
Searching
In the
Dark
and Dismal
Spots.

His prey is not
what a cat can eat.
But
Anything
That
Rots!

Proudly
to the Master's Home
he drags his
Useless
Prize.

The Master
Always
Disapproves.
The Cat,
He
feigns
Surprise.

Shaped by the Source

Casting my mind to discover the heart
Asking the heart to give life to my art.
Reaching for answers and questions and such
Finding the blessings that come with a touch.
Seeing the purpose and pain in my tears
Knowing I'm shaped by the source of my fears.

Casting my mind to discover the heart
Feeling the need to find peace in my part.
Asking the heart to give life to my art
Wondering how far I've strayed from my chart.

Reaching for answers and questions and such
Straining for life and keeping my crutch.
Finding the blessings that come with a touch
Hoping the power's just enough, not too much.

Seeing the purpose and pain in my tears
Adding up losses as the end appears.
Knowing I'm shaped by the source of my fears
Knowing I'm shaped by the source of my fears.

Feeling the need to find peace in my part
Wondering how far I've strayed from my chart.
Straining for life yet grasping my crutch
Hoping the power's just enough, not too much.
Adding up losses as the end appears
Knowing I'm shaped by the source of my fears.

The Stroke

The stroke imposed itself on us, a guest not sought or
wanted
It pushed itself into our lives and every thought it haunted.
At work, or play, or quiet time, at table, chair or bed,
Not only in the victim's mind, the stroke was in each head.

The stroke pushed off each thought of peace, it entered
every prayer
It crowded out the chance to laugh and welcomed in
despair.
It showed the folly of a plan and destroyed normality,
A thing as small and quick as thought... exposed mortality.

The Lost is Found

We shouldn't be ashamed to say,
Although it's sad to count the cost,
That some will stay were they belong
And others, sadly, will be lost.

And though we wish to each unite.
And help the lost and found align.
It surely can't be eas'ly done
And takes an awful lot of time.

But what a joy to have a hand,
To help the lost refind their rolls,
Thus sorting out the diff'rences
That cover up our naked soles.

So put aside your daily cares...
Don't question - Don't even ask it!
Just put together all the odds
Found in your laundry sock basket.

Grief is Underrated - Overlooked

We think it only happens when a loved one dies.
But in the course of every day life
We lose some thing we cherish,
Some expectation flies,
A hope is shown vain,
Or friendship fails,
A trust betrayed.
And so we
Grieve.

And each grief we suffer and survive
Schools us for the greater blows
That life and death mete out.
And add to us a measure
Of compassion,
And of power
Unfound in
Sheltered
Lives.

A Pioneer Summary

On the eve of the big day for pioneers,
After a meal of barbecued pork tenderloin,
Rice, fried mushrooms, garlic toast,
Cauliflower smothered in cheese, fresh salad,
Candied carrots and onions, strawberries
And rhubarb cobbler with ice cream,
My sister told us that her daughter
Was speaking in Church that day
And had called her up to ask for
A simple story to summarize
The real meaning of being a pioneer.

"That's easy" my other sister said,
"You remember that when Grandpa Ackroyd
Was on his mission his pants wore out.
And that he went into the woods and
Sewed his hat into the seat of his pants,
So he could continue with his mission."

"That says it all." I agreed, suppressing a burp.
"It doesn't matter that technically speaking
Grandpa Ackroyd wasn't even a pioneer.
Let's break out those macadamia nut cookies,
The bridge mixture, and some grape and Ginger Ale punch.
Do ya wanna play Rook or Dominoes?"

Weeds and Seeds

If you study the garden, the gardener is shown
"By their fruits" it is written, "They shall be known".
Does this steward take care of his own every day
Or does he fear this work interferes with his play?
Does he humbly and quickly remove every weed
Or is he distracted, letting weeds go to seed?
It takes not a moment to give answer to this
And the proof of the harvest will show what's amiss.
No secrets can abide in the gardens we tend
Our neglect is exposed from beginning to end.
If you study your garden does it beg for your care
If you study your garden, in its need were you there?

Canto One:

My strength and my heart and my will
Failed in turn to meet my great need
And with patience and humbleness, still
Was my quest just expression of greed?
I was left in great doubt and despair
Unworthy, unsure and confused,
I came finally, only, to prayer.

And another was similarly bruised
Betrayed by someone who ought not
To have left him so cruelly abused
Wounded, believing all goodness forgot
Poisoned by drinking from a cup so unfair
Unworthy, unsure and confused,
He came finally, only, to prayer.

Two heartfelt prayers heard by One
And answered together, at once, by a Son.
Joining in joy what misery had made
Erasing the pain of being betrayed.

Canto Two:

Some paths are designed to ease us along
To avoid what is hard and has danger
But other roads seem... our way to prolong
Designed only to bring us to anger.
We journey along such a difficult route
To test us or wound us severely
And weaken our faith and build up our doubt.

And drive us to madness nearly
And when such a way, prepared to dismay,

Marks success not by journeys completed
But by number of travelers that turn away,
You can know it's road by men meted
To test us and wound us severely
And weaken our faith and build up our doubt.

But the hand of the Lord can make straight a way
That indifferent men use to capture their prey
And untie the knots that entangle our lives
As we twist along evil men's dismal contrives.

Canto Three:

When we're blessed by a gift that's sublime
When our heart's true desire is attained
We exult and we thank, and we cheer for a time
And we treasure the thing that we've gained.
And if we are wise we recognize the source
Of the joy and the love we have found
And we pledge to adjust and to refine our course

To the strait and the narrow profound
And we keep in our minds every day as we can
The notion that we have been blessed
And welcome new problems and hurdles
And accept them as part of life's test
Of the joy and the love we have found
And we pledge to adjust and refine our course.

For the hand of the Maker is ever our stay
To patiently teach us in his loving way
And bringing together the lonely of heart
By clearing the paths that keep them apart.

How Does It Feel

"How does it feel when you're there?" asked the man
As he casually brushed back his hair.
"Whadduya mean?" says I with a grin.
Not wanting to encourage him.
"How does it feel when you're there?" he repeated
And patiently locked on my stare.
"It's the first and best test of what's good."
And he froze me right there where I stood.

Coralee and Katie

The hymns we sing are full of hope and lift my prayer to
heaven
Surrounded by the ones I love, this music works like leaven.
I know the organist by name, I've watched her since that
day
When she was given "Coralee" and blessed upon her way.

I've seen her learn to creep then crawl and then to learn to
walk
I didn't miss too many words as she learned how to talk.
I noticed as she grew and ran and kicked and threw a ball
An easy smile and happy eyes marked her as she grew tall.

Her virtue shone before her face and she grew strong and
lovely
And honour gave abundantly to parents, friends and
family.
She learned the art of working hard and walked the halls of
learning
Her modest life and sacrifice bespoke of bridled yearning.

And if I cast my eyes aside from where sits Coralee
I'll see a man who watches too, with babe upon his knee

I'm sure like her, he doesn't know my interest in his wife
And why I've fondly followed her at every stage of life.

He might, this day of straining hymns that cry from out
her hands
Consider that my teary eye was raised by holy plans.
And he would in a general way be close upon the mark
Not knowing that my mind has been considering the dark.

And thinking of another babe brought forth for name and
blessing
That very day with Coralee, a Father's love expressing.
A babe who never learned to run or talk or jump or swim
A babe whose early destiny was to return to Him.

So pardon if I seem too much to notice Coralee
I hope it doesn't bother you, it isn't her I see.
It's only just a way I've found for almost thirty years
To lift a father's heavy heart with shades of what may be.

Flint in the Grass

As we walk through the grass
My feet tell me the ground
Is as hard as flint.
"Why won't it rain? Why?" I cry.
"Why don't you ever water the lawn?" my wife says.

The Serpentine Vines

Silently he lay on his back
Head down against the earth
Holding his breath
Listening.
He thought he could hear
the pumpkin vines as they stole across the grass,
Serpentine, yet with sticky fingers
Grabbing whatever they touched,
Stopping only to bloom
and cast out fruit full of terrible seeds;
Then slithering on through the fence.
Yes, he could hear them growing,
Creeping, grasping, climbing
And he wondered why,
Why were were they so vital,
so fecund and so greedy
All at once?

And when he drew his breath
he could no longer hear the vines
but tasted the smoke in the air.
Smoke carried on the wind
from fires hundreds of miles away.
Smoke that burned his throat,
Stung his eyes, and blocked the light.
Filling his lungs with doubt.
The product of death, he thought.
The proof of death.
"Ashes to ashes" he said as he
lifted his head.

Hurray for Wednesday

Hurray for Wednesday
The middle child of the week
It's in the valley not the peak
Not flashy or boisterous
Not pious or cloisterous
A get the work done day
A hamburger bun day
Not much of a fun day
Still Wednesday's the one day
(Not Friday or Sunday)
'Tween Tuesday and Thursday
A just kind of occurs day
It's in the valley not the peak
The middle child of the week
Hurray for Wednesday.

Workin' Yer Plate

"It takes three cobs of corn like that to satisfy me." he said,
and he pushed his knife forward between his thumb and
forefinger.

"And I like to cut off just a bit at a time like this." he
continued as he carved a short curved stroke through the
air with his knife.

"Then I mix a teaspoon of hot corn with a teaspoon of
butter. Mmmmm."
And he closed his eyes with a trace of reverence in his
voice.

"That's the best way I've found to eat corn on the cob." he
concluded, and I wiped my chin across my shirtsleeve and
thought about it.

That Cat

That cat is bigger than the rest
He makes a lion cower
He stands above the king of beasts
With majesty and power
His tracks are like a garbage lid
His scent's not like a flower
His legs are long as anything
He stands up like a tower
His ears are big as elephant's
Each note he sings is sour
His eyes can penetrate a fog
He'll see you, then devour
His muscles bulge along his back
His mouth is fixed in glower
He's taller than a camel
And he grows more every hour
His breath is strong and wet and thick
And sprays like April shower
His shadow fills a normal house
And demons will empower.
That cat he seems to have a neck
As long as any broom
And his dirty coat is matted
Like he's never seen a groom
I do not know the name of that
That feline in my room
I've never heard before of him
From this I might assume
That I have just imagined him
He's not a source of doom
And when this night has finished
A bright new day will bloom
But just in case I'd like to ask
Dear daddy, in this gloom
If I may crawl in bed with you

And then I will presume
That awful cat will stay away
And save me from my tomb
So daddy let me in, I pray
And sleeping, I'll resume.

The Grizzly Blessing

Two hundred yards below us there
The lake was wild with bear
She crashing, splashing, lunged about
And showed no sign of care.

Her cubs were three and kicked around
Enjoying their wild delights
A family on a hot, hot day
In shoreline water fights.

When suddenly the grizzly sow
Sniffed danger in the air
And ceased her playful water games
And aspect turned to glare

Then gathered up in frantic chase
Her cubs along the shore
And snarling, snapping, pestering
She led them with her roar

They plunged in file into the trees
Away from crystal lake
And shortly reached a river wide
And swam to make escape

The mother drew from torrent strong
On distant river shore
Then each cub, in a perfect line
Along the forest floor

She turned and raised and threw
The water from her coat
And lifting up her mighty paw
With solemn growl in throat

She laid that heavy mother's hand
In turn on each cub's head
Counting. Blessing. One. Two. Three.
Then off to fate they fled.

The Boolean Blues

I got the Boolean Blues
I got the Boolean Blues
Just when I think my set is full,
You leave and I become a null
I've got the Boolean Blues.

I got the Boolean Blues
I got the Boolean Blues
Just when I think we'll intersect
Our union you will unelect
I got the Boolean Blues

I got the Boolean Blues
I got the Boolean Blues
I plan our little complementation
But then our elements you ration
I got the Boolean Blues

Out of the Grove

Oh mysteries of earth and fire and rock
You nevermore will be to us the same
The very dust now quickened to unlock
The truth which sets an honest heart aflame.

The trees that saw the boy step humbly in
And stood in wonder as they must have felt
At least a part of what would now begin
When just a boy in prayer so faithful knelt.

In shadows were his boyish features caught
His mission one to overcome a doubt
Then light in pillar blazoned overwrought
A boy steps in. A prophet's coming out!

So Joseph's face returned to morning light
Out of the grove. And now! The end of night.

Try to Remember

Try to remember
This time, in September
Try to remember
How many children?
So many children....
Each child and his age
And that child's learning stage.
And which child has no shoes
And what each child needs to use.
Every child and her books
And her clothes, and just how she looks.
Cause if you fail to remember
This time, in September
You'll feel such a fool -
It's the first day of school.

A Part of Me Has Gone Ahead

A part of me has gone ahead
And shares no more this pain
Is free from earthly fear and dread
Is purified from stain.

That part has earned its heavenly end
And leaves a lighted course
For all of me to find the rend
'Tween here and heaven's source.

Fear of Falling

I've walked these stairs a thousand times
Where Jesus walks and spirits dwell
Yet on this night I'm struck with fear
Of falling down the circled well.

The oaken railing strong and firm
Protects against a casual fall
No accident can take me down
I'm safe behind this railing wall.

My fall can only happen if
I willfully across it lunge,
Past circling rail and down the well,
A quick, and far, and deadly plunge.

The fear won't last but questions stay.
What force could tempt to even fear
This way that symbolizes best
The climb from earth to heaven's sphere?

When climbing with my face to heav'n
I never fear a fall at all,
It's in descent these fears appear.
When leaving home. I fear the fall.

The last few times I've noticed that the air rifle competition is typically finished even before the opening ceremonies begin. This got me thinking, what if I was in the Olympics.....?

If I Was In the Olympics

If I was in the Olympics
I'd skip all those sports where you run,
And is there really anyone
Who thinks weightlifting is fun?
I wouldn't ride horses
Or swim
Or throw spears,
And any game featuring balls,
Well that would just drive me to tears.
And I don't like to waste all my time
For me, a long ceremony is worse than a crime.
So if I was in the Olympics
Of all the events only one
Do I think would be really fun,
I'd shoot an air gun
And when I was done
And my anthem was sung
I'd collect what I'd won
And go home on the run
Before the ceremonies even begun.
That's what I'd do if I was in the Olympics.

Savage Digging

In the dry hot mid day summer sun
the surface of the cool dark clay
quickly frosted into white sand.
Sand that stuck to sweaty arms
and foreheads and collected
on the necks above their bare backs.
But no one noticed that,
not that or the smeared
dirt on knees and elbows,
Or the gritty accumulations
in their noses, teeth, hair or
the corners of their squinting eyes.

Without noticing or caring or thinking
the boys burrowed their way down,
Down into the earth,
By turning it inside out,
Upside down.
Exposing the mystery of the
underground and making the
common ordinary surface of the world
vanish.

Digging this hole was
creative and destructive,
It was new, it was ancient
It was thoughtful, thoughtless and
instinctive.

Shoveling in their ill suited shoes
Grunting, laughing, learning,
sometimes talking, sometimes
holding their peace.
Testing their strength, mastering
their tools,

These savage boys
Digging a hole for nothing,
Digging a hole today and
leaving it forever tomorrow.
Just an empty hole,
collapsing on itself,
poorly planned
and crudely built,
but proudly done.

Haiku?

Lifting my hand up
Against the light of the sky
My eyes wide open.

 Long shadows appear
White fields, ready to harvest
The frost before light

Thoughtlessly he said
I think not! And proved his point
The haze descended

bigger than a star
shining on the whole village
rice is everything

blood and bone and flesh
in the air by grassy knoll
bright red on pink dress

rusty spotted screech
burrowing snowy masked barn
who who who who who?

cold steel burns the hands
snow crunching under the feet
licensed to take life

Rain hiding the sun
The sheep lie in Green meadows
How about Haiku?

Old frying pan
The frog legs sizzle
Just like chicken

Temptation

I'm crossing ground that's beaten down
Where unseen souls in vast patrols
Have passed along, both weak and strong
In journeys blessed and journeys cursed
With open hearts and grudges nursed.

I'm riding on a wave of song
That ancient spring was taught to sing
The siren air of temptress' fair
Both sound and sight both day and night
I'm lured by shadows and the light.

And still that's past, not future cast
My track is mine alone in time
In glory or in dark explore
I'll only be the path I see.
Because of this I'm new, and free.

A Sea of Glass

A sea of glass
Deep and cold
Drawing me in
Holding me near,
Gathering all
The afternoon light
Which warms the black rocks
Where I sit and reflects off that sea
In a blinding display of
Of serene and blazing
Mystery.

A sea of glass
Hiding secrets
But giving hints
In clear endless
Living waters,
Of distant harbours
Where glass bottomed boats
Lie at anchor disclosing the forbidden art
Of that which lies below
The fiery
Veil.

A sea of glass,
Maternal, all,
And everlasting,
Earth's great
Unfathomable
Breast, ready to
Nourish and comfort me,
Forge me as an iron link between an
Unforgiving earth and
A loving
Sun.

Here's my pretend review of a pretend book of poetry. It was fun to write, so I wrote it.

Review of "Dancing in the Wind"

The third book of verse by Andrew Gailey is called "Dancing in the Wind". It is in paperback only and is published by Intercity Press in Idaho Falls, Idaho, and was released on April 1, 2000 with a suggested retail price of $14.99. His
first book, "Never Hit the Nail" was a slight volume that had one small publishing run and is very hard to find. It introduced Gailey as a promising Mormon poet. That was in 1972 just after his early unexplained release from a mission in Missouri. I think my vote for most memorable poem from that volume would be "Alarmed". Since it's so difficult to find, here's a bit of that poem to remind you of it:

Out of my head
In the distance of sleep
Out of my pain
In the rattle of shame
Killing my soul
Alarmed I awake.

And then there was that more substantial offering:

Cords of Death

It first was born inside his heart

A deep, forbidden, blinding thought
Of sweetness with uneasy quest
So small and weak it threatened not

But crowded still and begged to grow
Against that host of better ways
His heart had safely harboured there
A curious conquest of his days

So soon! The seed was sprouting wild
Invading thought and sight and sound
A single thread of careful art
So loosely 'round his heart was wound
Cords of Death

He only felt its tug and pull
When instance of resistance came
And tightened all the casual strands
To purpose, these intentions tame.

And curiosity in turn
Became a course of learn'd desires
Which braided into strings of black
Untempered by these evil fires

Until the harmony of noise
And images of hopeless flight
And cruel habit's iron cords
Imprisoned him in basest night.

In his second book, "I'm Asking" published in 1988, Gailey
showed more maturity, but less certainty as he seemed to
wrestle with the conflict of making a living, raising a
family and fitting it all together with gospel and church
responsibilities and doctrines. At times he resorted to
outright lament. Sometimes sarcasm got the better of him.
He has a sense of humor too. Who can forget his poem, "The
Ward Auction" from that book? Here's a few lines from it.

The Bishop's wife is holding high
my chocolate cake
While brother Smith pleads for bids
from a noisy crowd
All green with Jell-O.

70

And children run in frantic packs
throughout the church
While sister Lacey pleads for them
to "settle down"
All green with Jell-O.

Now Gailey is pushing 50, living in Hamilton, Montana
and teaching High School English to the disinterested
children of forestry workers, ranchers and those
commuting to Missoula. He seems to have given up
completely on taking his
primary inspiration from people and he finds his muse by
drinking in and describing the beautiful landscape of rural
Montana. This book has taken an interesting and
promising premise or challenge. He writes a poem for each
day
of the year based loosely on what that day presented him
for visual stimulation. Happily he has wound into the
many faces of a Montana year deeper, universal issues of
life and truth. His art has truly matured and his voice is
now clear and provocative. Here's the title poem of the
volume, written for October 9th.

Dancing In the Wind

Once glad cousins
pliant and green,
Now brittle and bright
Dancing in the wind
Beneath naked trees.
Hastily shouting
as they retreat
into the into lees and eddies
Where they silently
forgetting their lofty
beginnings,
Sleep together.

71

This simple description of the falling and dying leaves of autumn has to conjure up comparisons with our own physical and social demise. One sees that Gailey himself knows that Hamilton, Montana has surely become a "lee" for him.

One of the interesting departures for Gailey in this new book is his willingness to use different poetic forms. Surprisingly, his poem for December 25 for example, is a limerick:

This day brought a bitter wind singing
A carol of hopelessness bringing
A harsh cruel chorus
Attacking our forests
So wild it concealed church bell ringing.

If you read Gailey's poems to discover his faith you will not be disappointed. Confused perhaps, but never disappointed. He is never afraid to use his observations of nature as a springboard for exploration of issues of faith. At times, as in the limerick above, coming on such a significant day, he seems to say that nature is much greater, much stronger than any human notions of
religion or faith. But other times he expresses his testimony of transcendent powers. Still he holds to the metaphorical exploration, keeping his observation of nature preeminent. You may be blessed as you read his work, but you will never feel like you have stumbled into a versified testimony meeting. As a foil to the Christmas offering, here's what he wrote for April 6. Again exploring another form.

I know the night can't take it back
My hope of spring in blossom young
Bright colors crest the prairie hills
To prove the love of heaven's sun.

72

I know the night can't take it back
These fruitful signs will grow and grow
Until the night itself succumbs
To lasting summer light below.

Each reader will have to judge if this idea of a poem a day,
projecting the weather and the landscape into the heart
and soul works for them. It certainly works for me.

Prolonging

I read today that they've made a pill
To cure the common cold.
And now we have minoxidil
To keep a man from showing old.

And stomach ulcers go away
They heal with antibiotics.
And even pain won't often stay
When confronted by narcotics.

And if I'm feeling very sad
I can take a dose of Prosac
Or even Valium I have had
To change a mood that's black.

Still others claim a sip of wine
Or a single daily aspirin
Will keep the heart a beatin' fine
And arteries from collapsin'
Ya gotta love this modern route
With medicines that makes ya stronger.
But do they really help us out....
Or just make our misery longer?

My Cheesy Thanksgiving Poem

We have given our thanks
On this Thanksgiving day
By a marvelous feast
In the suitable way.

It was good, it was great
It was really quite fine
And it showed front to end
That we knew how to dine.

We began in the way
That tradition requires
With a huge roasted fowl
For our turkey desires

It was stuffed from both ends
With such glorious treats
Breaded stuffing in back
In the front, sausage meats.

We were happy the juice
Tasted great for our gravy
Cuz we had just enuff
To make float a small navy

With the taters well mashed
And the broccoli steamed
And the cute Brussels sprouts
Dressed in onions and cream.

Sweet potatoes and carrots
And black olives and pickles
And a cranberry sauce
Would give taste buds the tickles

With fresh rolls still so hot
They were dripping with butter
All of this and the pie
Made my heart quite aflutter.

But a mystery came
Just an hour perhaps
After cutting the pie
And beginning our naps.

When the boy of this house
Who is seems isn't much
For the sprouts and the olives
And the stuffings and such

After giving his thanks
With appropriate "please"
He requested a snack....
"Macaroni and cheese."

I Shot a Bird

I shot a bird and watched it fall
It's feathers caught the morning sun
A bit of blood, a quiet heart
A painful sign of what I'd done.

A Picture at an Old Soldier's Funeral

Nineteen years old
Tall and strong
Flashing a pirate's smile
He props himself
Confidently, carelessly
Against a flag pole
Standing with his legs crossed
Bravely facing the camera and
Wearing the uniform
Of his country.
Proud as a king
Incurably
Handsome
Hopeful
Honest and
Daring.
His mother's son,
His lover's one,
Freshly trained,
And ready
For war.

The Bow

Suspending, grasping, that which none can ever hold
A sign of hope and love and promise made of gold
Whose end is patient legend waiting to be told
Defining daylight's edge as holy hues unfold,
An open miracle in plainest sunlight bold
Sacred, kind and nourishing of hope
Exceeding mind and earthly scope
Illusory it mimes an actual slope
Defying that with which we cope
Obscuring lightly where we grope.
Keep the sign this prism broadly sends
Great awe and wonder truth upon us lends
Remember this against a sign of baser trends
Shout and sing hosannas, give glory while it bends
And ponder all that's possible, between the rainbow ends.

In Solitary Wonder

In solitary wonder
I stand in rooms where unseen thousands
Have trod this sacred ground
And where the echoes of their passing
Resound.
In solitary wonder
I stand in rooms where unseen thousands
Await to be unbound
And where the echoes of their waiting
Resound.

The still and lonely
Hopefulness of melancholy thought
Exalts in what has happened here
And grasps at what our God
Has wrought.

Malchus (Luke 22:50-51)

The man put his hand before his face and examined it
Then put it back to his ear and rubbed it
Then looked again.
It was normal, perfectly normal
The blood was gone
The pain was gone,
And he felt to cry out
To express his astonishment
To ask... to demand...
An explanation.
But instead he sank to the ground,
One minute he was in a terrible
Angry battle, fearing for his life
And injured, perhaps mortally,
And feeling the great power of
Indignity and duty
And importance,
And the next minute
He felt only weakness,
Wonder and insignificance,
He was used up, limp, stunned.
"What is happening?" he said to himself
Mouthing each word carefully,
Trying to make his
Mind make sense of this night.
He looked up,
"What is happening?" he said aloud
"What happened to me?" he cried out.
But there was no one to hear him.
No one to answer his question,
It was quiet all about him
The press of men and officers
Had moved on,
Taking their prisoner
Into the night,

Leaving this solitary man
Kneeling in the dark beside the garden,
Without a lantern or a torch.
Healed from his wound,
But in more pain
And confusion than he
Could bear.
A solemn unwanted, unwilling
Confused witness
To a miracle.
Now he grabbed clumsily again
At his ear, then looked at his hand again,
And in the bit of moonlight
He saw what looked like a heavy wet,
Stain of blood
On the sleeve of his cloak.
It was sticky to his touch.
He felt his ear again
Carefully, curiously, cautiously
Caressing this time
With his bloody fingers,
As he might now,
Every day
For the rest of his life.

I Hear a Prophet

I hear a prophet
A trumpet
Clear toned, mellow and deep
Polished and strong
In tune with the ancients
And cutting through today's noise
Calling out the notes
The rhythms and the melodies,
Calling out and blending in
Leading and sustaining,
A horn, a bugle, a siren
A beacon, a warning
A love song
Full of hope
Full of faith
True in every key
Sweet and enticing
I hear a trumpet
I hear a prophet.

Hats

Why is that man
In his Sunday
Go-to-meetin'
Gray wool suit
And red tie
Wearing a bright
Blue ball cap
With the logo
Of a popular
Herbicide on it?
...Why not?

I See a Cloud

I see a cloud
Arching across the mountains
Covering the evening sun
Firm against the wind
Defying logic
A sign of trouble
For some.

I see a cloud
Boiling mad
Hot and cold at once
Ready to pounce
To empty itself and run
A sign of trouble
For some.

I see a cloud
Dancing aloft
Playing at being
Making nothing into nothing
And then going away to no where
A sign of trouble
For some.

My List

I think I'll put tapioca pudding on my list
I'll slide it right there between smoked oysters
And grapefruit sections in light sweet syrup
I'm talking the pearl tapioca
Home made with
Big fish eyes
Real big!
In sweet egg yolk custard
Stirred to a boil,
Add lots of vanilla.
Fold in the beaten whites if you want,
(I can take that or leave it
But it keeps better if you don't.)
I'll put tapioca pudding on my list for sure.
Now, let's see,
What else should go in my 72 hour emergency kit?

Line Upon Line

Today I made a single scratch
An etch, a notch, a gentle mark
A smallish point of no import
No fire. At its best a spark.

But still, although the act was small
It took full measure of my art
My power, love and duty call
And of my focus, strength and heart.

And I will not accept that judge
Who views alone what was my day
But ask of him and you and me
To see it's place along the way.

And take my simple humble scratch
Perhaps for effort only blessed
And leave the judgment to the last
When every line has come to rest.

The Moon

The moon I see is hidden well
Though naked as I best can tell
Her modesty is kept in part
By shadows at her very heart.

She shines a pale and lifeless light
Unseen by day and weak by night
And so she rips at tide and flood
And shares her time and space with blood.

Her powers blessed with mystery
Untamed by force or history
She rides our skies both near and far
And shrugs at every twinkling star.

She makes her plea to men seduce
And binds them tight without excuse
A shadow destiny for some
Who fail to look and see the Sun.

Maternal Blindness or Insight?

A mother sees more in her child
Than a stranger's eyes can view,
A mother sees less in her child
Than is seen by me or you.
A mother sees weakness in some
That she never perceives at home,
And a mother won't see in another
The strengths that she finds in her own.

A Love Poem

I hope there's Lima beans in heaven
And fresh hot buttered rolls and jam
I hope there's barbecue and chicken
And scalloped potatoes served with ham.

I hope the table's set with silver
I hope we drink from crystal too
With gravy boats and napkin rings
And soup tureens for hearty stew.

I hope there's candles on the table
And golden chargers at each place
And I like to guzzle fizzy grape juice
When I sit down to fill my face.

And while I'll find it quite divine
To feast on things I like to chew
What really counts the most for me
Is knowing I'll be there with you.

Where Is My Faith?

WHERE is my faith?
I'm searching all around
In the sky or on the ground,
Where can my faith be found?

Where IS my faith?
I had it just last week
Such games of hide and seek
For faith, are really bleak.

Where is MY faith?
I know you have your own
But just for now it's shown
That my own faith's wind-blown.

Where is my FAITH?
I need to chase away from me
The fears and doubts I see
And query where my faith can be?

Quel Demise?

Some slip away so easily
Like words we speak too breezily
You see them Monday on the street
Looking fine. Then Saturday... Six feet!

Some stick around infinity,
You're sure they've met divinity
But then you meet them in a store
Surprise! They never died before.

Yeah Sure

Remember how we used to just
sit around after the meeting
and complain about the guy?
Everyone took a shot
it seemed,
And then we all felt better,
Felt like we had done something.
But we had really done nothing
Just complained
and nothing changed
No one belled the cat
No one really did anything
And now this happens and
Yeah sure,
We may say
we did the
best we could
but did we?

This March

This march, so long and slow with steady step, then rest,
Will lull the mind and heart and dull the sense of quest.
And by the time we reach where sight of end should be
Our stumbling wreck has lost, the very will to see.
So dread of march's end, a burden we can't share,
Has done it's duty well and on the pathway there
Is cast from failing hands, now fearless of the test
That waits at end of trail, and gathers in the blessed.

Where Are You Going?

Look, you fools, look.
Look where you're going!
You are going where you look.
Watch, you fools, watch
Watch where you're going!
You are becoming what you watch.
You are what you watch.
See, you fools, see
See where you're going,
What you see, is what you'll be.
Be careful where you look,
What you watch,
What you see,
You fools.
You silly fools
Who think you can
Look one way and go another.

Asbestos I Can

I know I'll get sick if I tan
Or become a great tobacco fan
In this wor-ld where cancer
Is so often the answer
I'm just doing asbestos I can.

Reflections on Alma 5

Clean out yer ears
Its all about what ya hears
Clean our yer ears
And listen.
Sharpen yer eyes
Roll over and look
Before ya dies
Sharpen yer eyes.
And if ya can hear it
And if ya can see it
Why can't ya feel it?
And when ya feel it
In yer heart
Then get up and walk
Get up and walk
And join His flock.
Clean out yer ears
For heaven's sake
Clean out yer ears.

Cry for Love

I asked the man to tell me how
It came to be that he was now
Estranged from what he once had been,
And changed into the best of men.
He humbly smiled and drew his brow
Into a knot of studied thought
And wondering at the thing he'd wrought,
Then tossed the answer from his heart
As true and clear as master's art
I guess, he said, this thing was brought
About by God, from up above
Responding to my cry for love.

Of Course

Of course his taste for things
So fine and rare
Was out of place
In this stormy
Autumn air.

Of course his casual dance
So free and light
Was out of place
On this bitter
Winter night.

Of course his dark desire
So mean and strong
Was out of place
On this sunny
April dawn.

Of course his measured step
So crisp and grey
Was out of place
On this sultry
Summer day.

Walking

I quite agree with those who say
That walking is the better way
And hold we shouldn't take the car
Unless the trip is rather far.

In fact I've felt this way for years
Even before aerobic fears
Were all the rage and seemed correct,
Twas walking earned from me respect.

And so as I resolve this year
To never drive a walk that's near
I think of that short block to work
Or that half block from house to kirk

And state in voice that's strong not shrill
The kind that shows my iron will
Outloud so that I can't deny it
"This walking thing, I'm going to try it."

However as you know my friend
While virtue is my stated end
It's kind of cold and snowy yet
Good footing still a long shot bet.

Perhaps as winter gives it's way
To lovely spring and pleasant day
I'll venture out on all those walks
And suffer neighbour's knowing gawks

And feel superior to my pals
Who always drive in these locales.
Or better yet to make no fuss....
I'll learn to take the public bus.

Some (Reflections on Helaman 13:38)

Some push on string
or shoulder up
to rocks too big to move.

And seek for light
in sources like
the dark side of the moon.
Then look for love
with selfish eyes
and hearts far out of tune.
And waste their days
in sin and lies
convinced that they're immune
from what must come
when what we've done,
is brought to light of noon.
Then all will learn
that happiness
from just One Rock is hewn.

Things I Know

I made a list of all the things I know
I thought that as I aged the list would grow
And over time I've been a faithful guy
To keep my list in shape. But I ask why,
For all the things I've done and what's been said
I fix my list with gum but never lead.

Tempered

The ore we dig from out the earth
Is coarse and common, useless stuff
And needs refining or its worth
Stays hidden in a heart too rough.

And even then, when cleaned and formed
By molten, and then, grinding force
To be its best it must be stormed,
White hot! Then plunged into the source.

And thus from dross is steel seduced
And cunning tempered tools produced
And great and lovely dreams are loosed.
A shadow of the course of man

Refined and tempered in this span
According to an ancient plan.

Into the Wind

I know what it's like to walk into the wind
To fight to breath against it's force
To feel the tears blown out of my eyes
And dust and grit without remorse.

I know what it's like to walk into the wind
To feel its icy breath on me
And hold my cloak against a power
That torments any part that's free.

I know what it's like to walk into the wind
To catch my balance as I go
And lean against it's awesome strength
And doubt my might against its flow.

I know what it's like to walk into the wind
And know my solitary tilt
Can never hope alone to win
Against a power as strong as guilt.

Shadows

By keeping back what light could tell,
The shadows cast a dismal spell
Oh, would that I could understand
The myst'ries of a shadow land.
I can but guess the things that lie
In places that my eyes deny
Those shadows keep their secrets well
And seem an earthly sign of hell.
Still, notice in the things at hand
How dark can make the light expand
And truth may sometimes catch your eye
Because a shadow crossed your sky.

I Went Gathering

I went gathering
filling my arms
grasping with my fingers.
Holding some in my teeth.
Wanting them all with my eyes.
And spilling what I could not keep.
Wasting,
losing,
forgetting
so much,
and keeping only the very best.

Windy Doggerel

It's funny how this wind can make
A lot of things go shake and bake
Things that normally are cool
And stay in stasis as a rule
In windy times like this I find
Act like those rock and roller kind
In fact I've seen a thing or two
That might surprise a pal like you
And so because they gave me awe
I'll share with you the things I saw
I must report to start this list
Some flying objects gone a miss -
Of course we've come to know that sheep
May flounder some in water deep
And so it's odd to see them bound
Across a lake, or bay, or sound
Or if you think a flying ram
Or sailing ewe or sky high lamb
Is something strange and sort of rare
You haven't seen our moving air!
And what about those pick up trucks
Fly'n in formation just like ducks
Or have you noticed in the sky
A greyhound bus that's on the fly?
And still I think what makes our gale
A cut above... is fine detail
You know the sort of thing I mean
The way it picks your pockets clean
And packs the dirt into your ears
You nose and toes and muds your tears
I think the way it scours a field
And leaves it like an orange peeled
Or how it tears a car door off
Should rate at least a knowing cough
Or have you noticed what is done

When two car doors are open'd at one?
That clever wind will clean that coupe
Of every child or boy scout troop
Of course the birds don't mind a breeze
Unless it blows away their trees
And rolls their nests and eggs away
They'd look on that with some dismay
Except no birds can e're be found
Unless they bounce back on rebound
Cause though there's ease to fly here
It's easy cause you never steer
Yes flying here is such a snap
You just let go and then... why.. zap!
I've seen the wind pick up a lot...
Stuff traveling as quick as thought
And though the sky is full of things
That our west wind so nicely brings
Such things as normally stay put
And bother cause they're underfoot
Are not a lot of trouble here
Our yards are always fresh frontier
Although the fences would hold clutter
If every fence post didn't shutter
And blow away like all the rest
Like tool boxes and steam chest
Like cattle, horses and like pigs
Like logs and boards and little twigs
Like dogs and Fords and kegs of nails
And dust and fish and hay and snails
Oh nothing sticks when this wind blows
The wind picks up, and off it goes
Though I can say that nothing's lost
Cause even though it's been wind tossed
I'll say it now at end of day
You only see things fly one way,
And whether bird or rock or beast
It's flying fast, but always east.

A Child's Poem

Some children don't believe in soup
They think it's awful icky goop
And I know kids who won't eat fish
They'd rather gnaw upon the dish.
And many youngsters will not eat
A single meal that's made with meat.
And vegetables it must be said
Fill children's hearts with simple dread.
But there's one thing that seems to please;
It's pasta and that processed cheese -
Yes macaroni's liked so well
I do believe it casts a spell
Cause judging by its taste and smell
I'm sure it's what they eat in hell.

Tender Mercies

From
where I lie
against the warm earth,
I watch the infinite horizon,
straight and pure above ripe golden fields,
Below a sky so blue and commanding that I barely notice
A woman, dressed as a bride, approaching from the
distance.
I call out, and with the sun streaming through her hair
She walks happily towards me
Growing before my eyes
Her tender mercies
filling all the earth,
all the heavens,
and me.

So Average

Some people take up lots of space
And seem to almost fill a place
They crowd right up there, in yer face
So full and yet devoid of grace.

While other's seem to disappear
Although we know they must be near.
They hunker back and look sincere
So brave and yet they're full of fear.

But as for me I'm neither way,
Not shrinking nor a boor at play
In fact, of me I hope they say
So average yet he's still okay.

Don't Bug Me

Don't bug me when I'm busy like I am
Don't hassle me or send me any spam
Don't ask me to be helpful, kind, or clear
Can't you see I'm in a nervous breakdown here?

(Chorus - repeat wherever the urge strikes)
Can't you see ...
Can't you see ...
Can't you see ...
It should be plain, as plain as plain can be
Can't you see ...
Can't you see ...
Can't you see I'm in a nervous breakdown here?

Don't shake your finger in my face or chest
Don't even think my work is less than best
And don't be giving me that look austere

Can't you see I'm in a nervous breakdown here?

Don't wink or even think to roll your eyes
Don't whisper back and forth with all your spies
Don't violate my growing comfort sphere
Can't you see I'm in a nervous breakdown here?

Don't ever try to patronize or save me
Don't ever try to satisfy or praise me
Don't try to show you're caring or sincere
Can't you see I'm in a nervous breakdown here?

Reflections on Hebrews Chapter One

Our God who spoke to prophets in the past
Hath given us One greater far than those
The One who made the stars, the earth and skies
And built each house, each eagle, and each rose

Descended from His place at God's right hand
And came to earth in charity and love,
And bore upon his tender countenance
The image of our Father up above.

No angel ever was as great as Him
And prophets bow their heads before his face
His scepter is a mark of righteousness
That signifies his endless love and grace.

He purged all sin from every willing soul
By condescending lower than us all
His might to save and bless is infinite
He's Jesus Christ, the greatest one of all.

No Sonnet Today

The part of me that makes a sonnet
The part that's underneath my bonnet
Today has only nine beats on it.
That's why I cannot write a sonnet.

Knot Like That

Big frog
Little pond
Big bull
China shop
Big dog
Silly blond
Half full
Belly flop.

Picture
Thousand words
One way
Skin a cat
Stricture
Cut it loose
Cliché
Knot like that.

Redneck Love Poem - I Think

No mobile home or Trans-Am car
Compares with beauty like you are
No fish or bait or even Spam
Can match the smarts of how you am.
And cows and horses may look slick
But next to you they're kind of hick
And I once thought that well done steak
For simple beauty took the cake
But every time I think of you
I'm blessed with symptoms of the flu
And skies of blue and clouds of white
Remind me that you're out of sight.

Words That Rhyme with Smash

When all your assets turn to ash
And your insurance pays you cash
You may expect domestic clash
Before you buy a whole new stash
Cause if you're timid or you're brash
You can't determine in a flash
(At least to do so would be rash)
Just what to put in your new cache
So you should take some time and thrash
It out together over hash
So later on you will not gnash
Your teeth because in your slap dash
In order to resolve this mash
Without a slash or gash or lash
Your wants and wishes took a crash
Your fragile ego took a splash
And your new house got filled with trash.

This Ragged Day

This ragged day
torn from the fabric
of the steely
night.
Tossed into
the corner of the
heart and
lost from sight.
This ragged day
ripped wrung out
wiped up
and stained.

Sore Slack? Sit Back!

My feet are sore
My knees are slack
And if I sit
It pains my back.

That bear is sore
No time to slack
Let's not just sit
We should run back.

I have a sore
I'm feeling slack
That's why I sit
Here at the back.
My trials are sore
When will they slack?
Why can't you sit
Till I get back?

What's That?

I like to pay attention to...
What? Did you hear that?
the person that I'm speaking with...
What? Over there... Do you see?
and view an interruption as....
That's it! Over there. Over there.
more than just an unwelcome distraction.
Wow! I see it, I think I see it!

So I'll never let on that I ...
What is it? Boy is that loud!
even notice anything else
Awww... Wooo.. Look out!
because that would just be....
Okay. Okay. Let me get a better look.
so rude, you know....
Okay. Oh... never mind, it's nothing.

What did you say again?

Green

I feel a little GREEN
Not yellow or marine
I think I'll try steam clean.

I feel a LITTLE green
Not old, just seventeen
Life's not quite yet routine.

I feel A little green
It's not a kidney bean
But salad for the lean.

I FEEL a little green
A three putt's not serene
I'd rather not be seen.

I feel a little green
I've drank too much caffeine
Don't let me make a scene.

Brushing

With gum disease the agony
Can reach a very high degree
So recommended therapy
Should be obeyed religiously

So when the dentist said to brush
In light or dark, or loud or hush
I took my paste up in a rush
And started with a thorough flush.

I brushed my teeth from left to right
I brushed through day and into night
I brushed in crowds and out of sight
I brushed real hard, I brushed real light.

And then one day, just right at dawn
I checked the mirror with a yawn
And saw my brushing had wore on
So that, by then, my teeth were gone.

Temple Hymn
With sincerest apologies the Orson F. Whitney, who wrote the final stanza in 1923.

We love these rolling hills and grassy plains
Defended by great rocky mountain chains
And nestled in this little prairie town
A diamond fallen from the Father's crown.
So beautiful and strong its granite walls
So sanctified and pure its oaken halls
This sacred source of joy and much delight
A temple shining in our prairie night.

This home where dwells the Lord of light and life
This haven from a world of care and strife
Where angels witness every sacred rite
And each who kneels must wear the purest white
Where altars reaching up beyond this sphere
Remind of sacrifice, once made down here
We marvel at a gift so great and fine
A place, on earth, to sample the divine.

Hearts must be pure to come within these walls
Where spreads a feast unknown to festive halls
Freely partake for freely God has given
And taste the holy joys that tell of heaven
Here learn of Him who triumphed o'er the grave
And unto men the keys the kingdom gave
Joined here by powers that past and present bind
The living and the dead perfection find.

The Wind and Me

I was so lonely I sang with the wind.
Mimicked its shrill cry in the night
Howled as it howled in a storm
And whispered as it whispered
in the still, quiet, dawn.
And so we sang together through the day
and the night.
There was the wind and me,
There was always the wind
and only me.

When the Church Burned Down

When the church burned down
it took us all by surprise.
Such noise, such smoke, such heat.
And the winds blew in from the east
fanning the dancing flames into a frenzy.
A hypnotizing, wild, bright frenzy
against a dark low sky.
There was no rain but sparks
No relief, no stopping it until
it was all burned up.
The volunteer fire fighters
pumped water on the flames,
then on the ashes.
In the end only the pipes from the organ
rose from the rubble
mangled mute musical metal.
They would only stand for a few hours
and then the fire chief went to look at them
and somehow as he approached they became unsettled
and toppled into the rest of the charred muck
making a tinkling sound.

Lehi's Blues

Awake my sons; shake off those awful chains,
arise my sons: throw back those awful chains,
come on, my sons, why don't you use your brains?

Rebel no more against Nephi or Sam
don't turn your heart against Nephi or Sam,
just follow them, they'll lead you to the Lamb.

We must have perished in the wilderness
your bows were springless in the wilderness
but Nehpi's faith then blessed you nonetheless.

God said if ye will keep his each command
He says to keep his every command
that ye may prosper in this promised land.

A few more days and I go to my grave;
then who will pray your jealous souls to save?
Lehi's Blues Version II

Awake my sons; shake off those awful chains,
arise my sons: throw back those awful chains,
come on, my sons, why don't you use your brains?
Come on, my sons, why don't you use your brains?

Rebel no more against Nephi or Sam
don't turn your heart against Nephi or Sam,
just follow them, they'll lead you to the Lamb.
Just follow them, they'll lead you to the Lamb.

We must have perished in the wilderness
your bows were springless in the wilderness
but Nehpi's faith then blessed you nonetheless.
But Nehpi's faith then blessed you nonetheless.

God said if ye will keep his each command
He says to keep his every command
that ye may prosper in this promised land.
That ye may prosper in this promised land.

A few more days and I go to my grave;
then who will pray your jealous souls to save?
Then who will pray your jealous souls to save?

Be Satisfied

Oh lonesome cabbage on a hill
Cast off your dreams of coleslaw thrill
Don't pine for vinegar and spice
Be satisfied, you've got it nice.

Dear watermelon in your patch
Forget your plans to unattach
Don't lose yourself for other's needs.
Stay where you are and keep your seeds.

Oh lovely orange in a tree
Don't think you see yourself in me
It's fine if I do what I please
It isn't fatal when I squeeze.

And what about the lowly spud
He'd like a chance to leave the mud
Perhaps the army or the navy
Is where he'll learn to swim in gravy.

The Blues

You know the sound?
It crawls into your soul
and frees you from yourself.
You can make it with an electric guitar
or with a blues harp.
You just bend the note,
pulling ruthlessly on the stings with strong fingers
or abusing the reeds with tortured breath.
And that bent note
That tormented song
Claws at you, mimicking your pain,
until finally, everything is resolved.

Shopping Mall Lights

I choose to be buried between
The mall and a pure mountain scene
Behind the last parking lot fence
Where the pavement surrenders to green.
It may be a bit of pretense
To be finally planted out hence
But I long for the clean mountain air
Near the joy of a mall that's immense.
In death then I hope I will share
The pleasures that shoppers declare
As well as those outdoor delights
That in life I found utterly spare.
And looking down from the great heights
On most any clear late shopping nights
It'll be sleeping there quite dead to rights
In the glow of the shopping mall lights.

Against the Greatest Certainty

So many things a mile wide
Are only inches deep
So many dangers that seem dead
Are really just asleep.
We grasp and clamor for a share,
A piece of something sure,
A way to chase away our fear
And find a lasting cure,
We see we need some inner strength
Some source we all can trust
Against the greatest certainty:
This life is "dust to dust".

Lettuce Sing the Blues

Most singers never learn technique
They make a show of singing strong
But like the squash and like the leek
They usually get the music wrong.

Of course you have to have an ear
To sing with confidence and pitch
Perhaps that's why you'll always hear
That singing corn's in tune and rich.

And musicality demands
A sense of rhythm clear and sweet
That's why we choose to clap our hands
To rhythms laid down by a beet.

You have to have that special eye
To see how music fills your life
That's why, as hash or mash or fry
Potatoes tune with fork and knife.

I love to train a little choir
Of vegetables so fresh and green
And as their voices rise up higher
I'll oft forget they're just cuisine.

So Refreshing

I wanted to see down the well
into the ancient black
to see it's bottom
and wonder why
the cool air against my face
was so refreshing.
I wanted to see an angel
lift a poor scorned mother
to help her fill her bottle
for her son, the father of many nations.
I wanted to be at the well
to hear the crowds and see the quiet
stranger waiting for a damsel to offer
him water.... for his camels.
I wanted to hear a woman
agree to draw water for the Jew
and hear him teach her
and offer her living water.
I wanted to see down the well
into the ancient black
to see it's bottom
and wonder why
the cool air against my face
was so refreshing.

Joe's Pigs

I had a spell of sickness for a year,
The wife and kiddies hung in best they could
But I was out of work and filled with fear
'Cause bills kept piling up they way they would.

And when I felt a little more like me
I found a job and tried to pay my way
But I was far too deep in debt, you see,
And soon was wracked with guilt and with dismay.

I s'posed I'd hit the bottom pretty young
And couldn't see a way to dig back out
I felt my face was shaded from the sun
And lived in constant fear and hopeless doubt.

I don't know why I went to see the man
I'm sure it wasn't faith or hope or trust
I maybe only thought he'd understand
And validate my troubles as unjust.

He listened in an attitude of care
And heard my story all from front to back
And when I finished he began to stare
And made me wonder if he'd lost the track.

Then finally he asked a simple thing
A question which he knew the answer first
But one that in me made my tears to bring
And guess I'd prob'bly gone from bad to worst.

He asked me if I'd kept my off'rings straight
And paid the Lord His due from what I'd made.
I bowed my head and told him that of late
As he well knew, the Lord had not been paid.

I looked up in his eyes to see if then
He'd give me some excuse for my mistake
He knew that I had had it bad since when
I got too sick to any paycheck make.

But I looked for a pardoning in vain,
I guess somehow he knew that long before
I ever had the first of sickness pain
I'd held back quite a little on that score.

But as the mis'ry of my fault sunk in
The man said something, caught me by surprise,
"If you will from this moment now begin,
To pay the Lord his due I can advise,

"He'll open up the skies and shower you
With blessings greater than you've ever dreamed
And all those debts that now are over due
Will soon be satisfactor'ly redeemed."

I s'pose I might of doubted what he said
At least it may have seemed a little strange
But nothing else had entered in my head
To help me make my circumstances change.

So from that day I started playing straight
And paying to the Lord His honest share
And then I wondered just how long I'd wait
Before He chose to take me in his care.

I guess in just a month, or two ... no more,
While I was visiting a farm near by
Beside the farmer on his pig shed floor
I saw them in the corner of my eye.

They moved about like whispers in the wind
So strange and pale and slight and stumbling wrong

They're what becomes of pigs when you have sinned
And cannot feed them anything but song.

Could such a ghostly thing bring any good
These pigs too weak to live and near to death
I asked him why he didn't, if he could,
Release them from the misery of breath.

I told him I would do it as a balm
And shoot the critters gladly right away
To save them from that pain that lingers on
And hasten their inevitable day.

But then he said a thing that didn't fit
"I'd do it, but it just don't seem quite right
It isn't that I'm squeamish, not a bit
But somethin' tells me not to stop their fight"

He paused, and seemed to have a second thought
"Could you," he stopped again, "would you, for me,
Take care of all these starving pigs I've got?"
I made no answer to his fervent plea.

But asked instead what did he have in mind
And told him I could not afford to buy
And that I only wanted to be kind
And that these suffering pigs were sure to die.

He told me that he understood my plight
And that he knew the pigs could not be sold
And would I please just take them from his sight
It seemed a rather foolish plan, but bold.

"I'd love to help you, if I only could
But I don't have a truck or way to haul
And so this plan won't do you any good,
I'm sorry I can't seem to help at all."

He didn't bat an eye or hesitate
But simply told me he would haul the pigs
And so we quickly ended our debate
And I went home and waited for his rig.

My house was on a smallish village lot
And if a load of pigs should somehow come
I'd need to find a bigger better spot
To make these visitors feel right at home.

A neighbor through the back had extra land
And buildings from some former enterprise
And so I asked him if he ever planned
To use those vacant lots, the perfect size.

He said he had a feed lot there one time
For pigs, and that it worked out very well
He guessed for just that purpose it was prime
But that he wouldn't need it for a spell

And if I had a way to make some use
Of land and buildings as and where they stood
He'd sooner see his old feed lot produce
Than be reduced to weeds and rotten wood.

I told him that I couldn't really pay.
"No problem, I'll be happy just to see
The lot is back to working in some way
Perhaps you'll use it like it used to be?"

But on that weekend when the farmer's truck
Puffed in my yard to leave its porcine load
I saw at once that I was out of luck
The pig's were nearly dead that it bestowed.

I asked the driver just to take them on...
A place I knew behind a quiet hill
So I could help them to their fate foregone
Then fetched my gun to make the mercy kill.

But now a thing a little strange to say
The truck was weaker than it's humble load
For as it tried to rev and pull away
The motor seized before it reached the road.

And so I carried pigs too weak to walk
And placed them in the shed my neighbour gave
And started nursing them around the clock
To see if just a few I might not save.

And soon, I think before the truck was moved,
A man I hardly knew said he had heard
I had some pigs and that if I approved
He had some grain, though not the sort preferred.

It seems that little bugs were in the grain
And left it only fit for pigs or such
"But I can't pay for it!" I told him plain.
"Oh no! Just take it, thank you very much."

"I'd love to take it, if I only could
But I don't have a truck or way to haul
And so this plan won't do us any good,
I'm sorry I can't seem to help at all."

"No worry" said the farmer with a smile
"Just take my truck" he said. And tossed the keys
I s'ppose he knew he'd gone the "second mile"
And looked about happy as you please.

That buggy grain was more than we had guessed
I filled his truck up twice to get it all
And every pig ignored the buggy pest
And feasted on the grain spread in their stall.

Still grain that's whole needs chopping to be right
For pigs or livestock, feed should be a mash
And so I worked and worried in my plight
Because I had no way to chop or smash.

Another day, by now, I understood,
A fellow stopped and told me that he had
Just bought a feed mill that was new and good
And if I'd take his old one he'd be glad.

"But I can't pay for it!" I told him plain.
"Oh no! Just take it, thank you very much."
"But I can't even haul it" I explain
He smiled as he gave his truck a touch.

Well in those lovely pig sheds in the back
And feed delivered in the proper way
I soon forgot they'd ever had a lack
And watched them growing fatter every day.

Still as they grew beyond the proper weight
I wondered hopelessly if every pig
Would be too fat and miss his normal fate
Because the auctioneer said "They're too big!"

But without truck or trailer at my hand
I had no way to get them down the road
Until another man came by as planned
Inquiring about my transportation mode.

116

He'd bought a load of tools at a sale
That came as packaged in a trailer rig
But while he needed all the load detail
He thought the trailer perfect for the pig.

"But I can't pay for it!" I told him plain.
"Oh no! Just take it, thank you very much.
It's just a clutter in my farmyard lane."
And then he smiled and gave my arm a touch.

And so I hooked that trailer to my car
And filled it full of hogs too fat for sale
And 'cause the yard I visited was far
I prayed for human kindness to prevail.

The auctioneer, I guess, had seen me come
And ran to meet me at his saleyard gate
He acted like my oldest fondest chum
Unloading all my pigs at frantic rate.

It seems he had some buyers who were hot
To pick up pigs of any size or shape
And other sellers he, I guess, had not
And so he didn't want me to escape.

In fact he made me go back to my place
And fetch the whole of all pigs I'd fed
And when I'd finished up my final race
He paid a handsome dollar for each head.

That money paid up all my overdues
And set me up for peace of mind and heart
And then and ever after I will choose
To always pay the Lord his proper part.

117

And while I'm grateful for those many men
Who gave and didn't ask for any pay
I know my freedom started only when
I went to see the man that fateful day.

That day the mis'ry of my fault sunk in
And he said something, caught me by surprise,
"If you will from this moment now begin,
To pay the Lord his due I can advise,

"He'll open up the skies and shower you
With blessings greater than you've ever dreamed
And all those debts that now are over due
Will soon be satisfactor'ly redeemed."

The Angel

The last living angel
gently put his hand
on my shoulder
and threw his black hair back.
I looked into his
eyes for an instant
and he looked into
mine.
it's not too late
he said without words.
I tried to believe,
then brushed
aside his hand
and looked down.
He was gone before
I would dare look up
again.

The Gladiator

The gladiator swung the dinosaur
over his head and threw
it wildly into the air.
All around him we shrieked
and flinched
but the action figure fell
harmlessly to the floor.
Amused and intrigued by
this power to make adults cower
he quickly rescued it
and was attempting another
launch when his mother
snatched the weapon
unceremoniously from his hands.
Howling. Every aspect
disclosing his betrayal,
disgrace and
disappointment,
He retreated.
Bitter defeat for now,
But every champion
will return to battle
again when his enemies
least expect it.

How is the War Going
October 17, 2001

"Hey Mr. Taliban, tally me bin Laden"
How is the war going?
Rockets red glare
the bombs bursting in air?
Large mounds of coarse rubble
being reduced to large mounds of fine rubble.
"And when you've tallied him, tally me that Saddam."
How is the war going?
Stopping men in airports
Dropping leaflets and food packages
"Anthrax, two thrax, three thrax, Four!"
How is the war going?
Nasal swabs, mail room sweep
close the congress
treat the sick.
"Look where you can for the anthrax spore!"
How is the war going?
Smoke them out
get them running
hunt them down and bring them to justice.
"One plane, two plane, three plane, Four!"
How is the war going?
Boxcutters? What are those?
Stray missiles, brave captives
widows, orphans, canceled flights, canceled lives.
"One thing for sure, there's bound to be more."
How is the war going?
Smoke them out of their holes
Bring them to justice
Who are they?
"Daylight come and me wanna go home."
How is the war going?
Ground zero
memorial services, prayers and vigils

hoaxes and heroes.
"Daylight come and me wanna go home."
How is the war going?
Soldiers and sailors at work,
secret, deadly work,
endless talking heads and noisy violent demonstrations in
the
streets.
"Day, I say day, I say day, I say day, I say day...
Daylight come and me wanna go home."

Sweeping Up

I spoke at a funeral the other week. It was for a dear old
friend. She was only 72 years old and cancer was found in
her digestive system about 2 months ago. She went so fast.
After the ceremony, the interment, and the family dinner I
was pushing the huge dust mop brooms around the cultural
hall with the bishop (my wife is the Ward Relief Society
President, so I was doing my sworn duty as third
counselor) and I saw it. Perched on the end of the stage. A
picture of the deceased, age 17, posing with her
groom. She had graduated the day before as valedictorian
of her high school and got married with nothing else ever
in her mind or heart than to be that man's bride forever.
She had Hollywood beauty and he was just as handsome as
she was gorgeous. I was riveted to the spot, forgetting my
broom. He with his one hand on his hip and the other
reaching out to her. She doing a bit of a vamp, looking over
her shoulder into his eyes. Wearing a full
short skirt, flowing hair, a smile that hid nothing, and
patented dimples that would grace her face forever.

"Whatsamadder?" asked the bishop, waiting awkwardly for
me to catch up and holding his broom impatiently.

My Life

My life is beautiful
My life is green
My life is musical
My life's a dream

My life is beautiful
My life is bright
My life is comical
My life is light.

My life is beautiful
My life is fine
My life's angelical
My life's divine.

My life is beautiful
My life is droll
My life's unusual
My life is full.

My life is beautiful
My life is sweet
My life is quizzical
My life's complete.

The Race

In the race
to push string
up hill
in the snow
with our noses
I favor the
laid back approach.
Let the string
come to me
I say.
I'll just sit
here and
make a
comfy place
for it.
And
I will be one
with the string
in my own time.
Or not.
But you can
push ahead
if you want to.
Push ahead,
and win the
race.
All you can
ever really
win
is envy.
Any other
prize is just
an illusion.
Push ahead.

Reflections on Barbara Olson 1955-2001

She had a gift to smile.
Disarming charming.
A needle bleeding
all the pretentious power
out of solemn fools.

She had a gift to smile.
Engaging outraging.
Not waiting. Advocating
for life
and faith and hope.

She had a gift to smile.
Teasing pleasing.
A scamp, a champ,
for laughter and for law
and of the right.

She had a gift to smile.
Courageous contagious.
Disclosing and exposing
moral shadows
with light, and love.

She had a gift to smile.
Delightful insightful.
Endearing cheering
A gift of sharing, caring, and
not easy to forget.

(After 9-11 there was an outpouring of patriotism in the USA which was symbolized by car flags everywhere)

The Flag and the Duster

The flag was purchased by a sincere 10 year old with money she earned babysitting. She was waving it bravely out the window of the family Suburban as they whistled down the highway, and the whole family of nine was singing "My Country Tis of Thee" and sadly the flagstick, made in Taiwan, snapped at the height of the chorus and the flag flew out of her hands, fluttered ignominiously and violently to the pavement. Of course she called out for her father to stop the Suburban so they could rescue the flag from it's unhappy and inappropriate place, but at that very moment mother went into labor and the father had to choose between taking his sweetheart to the hospital and trying to stop on a busy Interstate and rescue the disgraced banner of liberty. As the family knelt in prayer beside the road to open a council to discuss this moral dilemma little Andrew, the second youngest boy, (the sickly one) began to suffer from an asthma attack. As Philip, the oldest boy, reached for Andrew's inhaler he noticed that Carline, the baby, was turning blue, having apparently inhaled one of the small parts of the 3D puzzle toy that had come with the Happy Meals they were enjoying as they drove along. Now things were desperate. The baby was choking, Andrew was wheezing, Cecilia, the oldest girl, was coaching Mama in her labored breathing, and the flag was still somewhere out there down the road. Quickly sensing the need to make an executive decision, the father abandoned the council and issued wise orders to his troubled family. "Frederick, you and Nathaniel will stay behind and recover the flag. We must not let our own simple troubles besmirch the pride of our nation. The rest of you, back in the Sub and we'll head for the nearest hospital". As he said this he slapped the baby vigorously on the back dislodging the puzzle piece and releasing the child from certain death. "We'll be back before the end of the week, he called out to Fred and Nat as he pulled away from the roadside and he tossed them each a backpack containing a roadside 72 hours kit. When you find the flag, you know what to do with it." And he breathed a prayer of thanks for good scout training. With that the family was gone and Fred, the brave 12 year old and his handsome 11 year old brother Nat turned back down the road looking into the gathering dusk for a sign of the red white and blue.

It takes a while to slow down and park one of those Suburbans and then it's not easy to pull over in heavy traffic and find a good safe place to stop, so they knew they had a good mile or more to go to find the flag. With the enthusiasm of youth, however, they shouldered their back packs, being careful to put both straps in place so as not to injure their growing spines, and set off on their quest. As each oncoming car flashed past them they braced themselves against the wash of air that inevitably unsteadied their pace. So they were somewhat ready for the consequences when a Peterbilt 18 wheeler, driven by Grafton Brooks III, a failed stock broker and scion of the infamous Brooks family out of Florence, Nebraska, passed by them in the outside lane.

Grafton was looking desperately for the next exit. He had seen the flag on the road and knew he would have to go back and rescue it, but he had a full load of Cipro for rush delivery to the New Jersey Postal Service and he had been give strict orders not to leave it unless he was able to park in a secure location. It would not do to park it by the side of the road. So his eyes were searching for an exit and he didn't notice the two brave boys hiking resolutely up the road. He didn't ever know that the wash of his giant truck would tumble them down into the ditch like two balls of cotton candy caught in a high wind. And of course, no one

126

knew that at that very moment an exuberant horn player
from the opera, distracted for a fateful split second, by
the process of composing a poem to the memory of patriotic
school children singing the national anthem, if not lustily,
at least shrilly, was delivering the coup de grace to the flag
as his 1972 Dodge Duster slid hopelessly across it. He had
hit the brakes, but it was too late, and the very effect of
locking his wheels as they crossed the flag virtually
vaporized the remnant of Betsy Ross's fertile imagination.

Hack in the Hack

*Hack
hog line
in turn, out turn, on the broom
sweep hurry hard clean off hard hard hurry hard HARD
get by the guard
raise double take out
in the house, shot, on the button
deuce, take one, steal, blank?
No. Eight ender.*

The Horseshoe

I'm not kidding,
They found a horseshoe in its heart.
Badly rusted, somewhat bent.
A large shoe for a large working horse
wedged in the heart of the
ancient, magnificent tree.
Incorporated by growth
and only exposed when
the wind blew last week and
sent the tree
crashing to the ground
in the yard of the cabin
built by Samuel.
Where he lived with his son
Heber and where later
Heber would live
with his son, and my
father, Grant.
They gave it to me,
(not the tree, the horseshoe)
and I love it, but I don't
know what to do with it.
I could put in the little
box with Samuel's silk scarf,
his two pen knives and
his leather bound penciled
diary. I can't put it
in the pocket of Heber's
wool dress coat in my
laundry room closet with
his name elegantly
signed on the label,
the pockets are worn full
of holes already. But you don't keep
a horseshoe in the house anyway.

Maybe I'll nail it to
that tree growing in my
yard and wait for the
tree to grow and the
wind to blow.

Jacob & Ezra (Reflections on Pride)

Consumption that's conspicuous
And pride that's now ubiquitous,
Begins within the heart of man
And ends with feeling "better than".
While Jacob saw this in his day
And Ezra pointed us our way
I fear it's only gotten worse
Since Satan opened up this curse.
We seek to please the world's eye
By what we wear, or own, or buy
Not thinking of the need to be
Submissive and in harmony.
It's not enough to have enough
Say's C.S. Lewis of this stuff
We always seem to keep the score
Of who has less or who has more.
We start and end with none of this
But in the middle we think bliss
Is found in what we have and hold
Exclusive from the common fold.
No wonder pride and sinful parts
Weigh heavy on the prophets' hearts
We seem so ign'rnant of this sin
Repentance therefore can't begin.
Until we see our fallen state
There's little hope, it will abate.
Let's flood our lives, as Ezra says,
With Book of Mormon messages.

Club President

I saw her walking down the street alone
and thought how she had golfed those years ago
trailing wild children, boisterous, laughing loud
and wearing high heeled shoes that marked the greens.
Her husband not there, just mom and the kids
and me the club president seeing it
and knowing I was trustee of the course
and that I would hear more of this breach
This violation of the laws of golf
And I did hear, but I don't think I did
anything about it. Just kept it close.
My prosecutorial discretion
I guess. And soon her man took an attack
dying even before all those children
could grow up and move away. I wonder
now as she walks and I drive by if she
still golfs, because I don't, and never have
at least not much, since I was president.

My Pledge (A Song of Sartorial Suffering)

I might scribble down a sonnet or a 34 page ode
I might scratch my silly bonnet dreaming up poetic code
I might write a hundred limericks before the break of dawn
But I'll never wear my blue suit when I've got my brown
shoes on.

Chorus: (as often as necessary, if ever):

No, I'll never wear my blue suit when I've got my brown
shoes on
That might be a fashion faux pas which would make some
others yawn
But for me I'd rather be changed to a duckling from a swan

*Than to ever wear my blue suit when I've go my brown
shoes on.*

*I might fight a thousand demons and more dragons before
lunch
I might eat a ton of garlic and upon raw tuna munch
I might saddle up a rhino or hitch up a new born fawn
But I'll never wear my blue suit when I've got my brown
shoes on.*

*I might talk when I am chewing and be loud when I should
not
I might sing along at movies and then give away the plot
I might ask a million questions that are dumb or even
wrong
But I'll never wear my blue suit when I've got my brown
shoes on.*

*I might wear a hat in chapel and forget to clean my nails
I might lie about my fishing and neglect to play my scales
I might order me a lobster and complain that it's a prawn
But I'll never wear a blue suit when I've got my brown
shoes on.*

*I might whine about the weather and forget to wear my
coat
I might put you in a trance because I smell just like a goat
I might make a mock of money or of guys whose names are
Sean
But I'll never wear a blue suit when I've got my brown
shoes on.*

*I might sing and stamp my feet until my toes are red and
raw
To the tune that we all recognize as "Turkey in the Straw".
I might marvel you with muscles and my manly burly
brawn*

But I'll never wear my blue suit when I've got my brown
shoes on!
No I'll never wear my blue suit. when I've got my brown
shoes on...
Never ever wear my blue suit....
No I'll never wear my blue suit....
No I'll never wear my blue suit, (big finish)
When I've GOT MY BROWN SHOES ON!
(conclude with the "shave and hair cut, six bits!" vamp -
"brown and
blue clothing, don't mix.")

Ties - A Rant

The use of a fine silk tie as a napkin has never appealed to
me from a convenience or economical point of view. But it
does bother me that a good tie costs twice as much as a
good shirt. The neck tie, or vestigial scarf, is certainly the
least favorite fashion accoutrement that I wear regularly.
Before I taught early morning seminary I usually chose
only to wear a tie on Sundays and on my temple day. I
would wear golf shirts the rest of the week. Now I'm in a
white shirt and tie everyday but Saturday. The long term
cerebrovascular effect must be severe, judging by the
frequent evidences of diminished mental acuity that dog
my path on a daily basis. I think it's a major cause of heart
and stroke disease, and cancer as well. In fact, if I didn't
know better I'd guess Islamic terrorism was largely an
outgrowth of the same phenomenon. Not to mention the
crash of Enron, and I even wonder if Mike Tyson doesn't
secretly wear a tie too much. While it may be too strong a
statement to blame all the ills of the world on neckties, it
has to be high on a list of visible contributing factors. Most
workers like to blame the "suits" in their companies for
most of their troubles. This blame is misplaced. It's the ties.

Your Eyes

You can take me as I am
You can take me as I am
Or you can take me...
With your eyes.

You can leave me as I am
You can leave me as I am
Or you can leave me...
With your eyes.

the devil's mirror

his heels struck the devil's mirror
crisp dark hard
lightening strikes
to wake the dead
and shake the living.
the devil raged
and poured his wrath
upon the striker,
unleashing lies
hate
and terror,
gathering his wicked
weaklings to stop
this man.
but the prophet's blows
had cracked
the mirror
and the work
had begun
and the devil's end
was sure.

I Like to Eat it All

(the first verse is a sort of chorus with a shorter meter that can be
added back into the song from time to time as desired)
I like to eat it all, not just the bread and jam
I like to eat it all not just the toast and ham
I like to eat it all. I like to eat it all.

When food is on the menu, as it often seems to be
What bothers me is just how darned selective I can't be
I like to eat it all, I like to eat it all.
Some people stick their noses up at vegetables and such
They fancy only foods prepared with fancy gourmet touch
I like to eat it all, I like to eat it all.
There's folks who're plagued by allergies and sensitivity
Those folks grow thin and pale and slight, but those folks just ain't
me.
I like to eat it all, I like to eat it all.
And I can say I never met a ham I did not like
And I was voted least of all to go on hunger strike
I like to eat it all. I like to eat it all.
I don't believe in prejudice I've been this way for years
I'm sure that's why as time went on I outweighed all my peers.
I like to eat it all. I like to eat it all.
I am a fan of stir fry, and of pork chops and fondue
Of cooking on the stove top, oven, or the Bar B Q
I like to eat it all. I like to eat it all.
And when I die I guess the guy who carries my remains
Will mutter as he lifts and puffs and tugs and blows and strains
He liked to eat it all. He liked to eat it all.

This Easter Morn

This Easter morn and Matthew 24
is more on my mind than Luke 24.
Earthquakes more than resurrection,
Wars and rumours of war more than peace,
Famine and pestilence more than fullness and healing.
The very earth shakes and men's hearts grow cold with
hate.
The time of sorrow is upon us.
The worst is yet to come
and so is the best.

Breaking Bread

In slow motion
a crust of bread
will explode when torn
sending fragments of life
shrapnel, pollen, living dust
spraying across through the sunlight
catching the beams
and flashing them
boldly for an instant
of comprehension.

Approaching the Harbour of New Orleans (1853)

The Ellen Maria sat proud in the water
Her sails all a billow, the Empire's daughter.
And farmers and printers and merchants and bakers
and tailors and spinners and tinkers and traders
were huddled on deck in the wind driven rain
with their wives at their sides in a fury of pain.
And the captain and crew stood apart but so still
that the company's prayer sounded lonely and shrill.
Then the gun fired thrice as salute to his days
and young Joshua's body slipped under the waves.
The Ellen Maria sat proud in the water
her sails all a billow, the Empire's daughter.

Approaching Saint Louis (1853)

Across the rolling river water
teased by moonlight leading nowhere
comes the sound of rough deck hands
ripping the night with liquor laden obscenities
and the steady pounding of the steam engine
as it relentlessly pushes the awkward craft up the river
and
in the background, weakly, as if miles away, but perilously
near,
if you listen intently, the cry of a newborn,
barely cleaned of the blood of birth
and held tightly to the breast of Elizabeth,
the exhausted mother.
They lie together on the open deck of the steamer
their only warmth the sleeping body of
Peter, the newborn's brother, as he cuddles
to his mother and coughs unconsciously in his sleep.

Approaching the Valley (1853)

*Two days from the Valley
anticipation thrilling every heart
and as if the wasted oxen
smelled the water of their new home
the company began to race,
if race is a word to be used
for people at the end of
1200 miles overland
and 3000 miles oversea.
But in a quiet wagon box,
oxen unyoked,
and grazing mindlessly nearby,
Elizabeth holds young Peter,
brother of Joshua,
cousin to Samuel,
in her strong arms and
weeps. One more who will
not see the Valley.
In this life.*

A News Haiku

*Trafficant gets eight
Pilot whales return to beach
Train goes off the rails*

How ya gonna go?

How ya gonna go?
In yer sleep,
in a fire,
in a fall?

How ya gonna go?
In yer car,
on a bike,
in a brawl?

How ya gonna go?
On a horse,
on a swim
in a squall?

How ya gonna go?
Might be sick,
might be quick,
you don't know.

My Gripe with Harper Lee

True you wrote the perfect book.
It helped me understand the need, sometimes,
to be angry and patient at the same time
It shone a bright light in a dark corner
and made a rushing noise in my heart
joining the powers of love, hate, innocence,
culture, the law, justice and family.
It was endlessly funny, rich, articulate,
sorrowful, hopeful, and enlightening.
You did it with the talent God gave you and
for that I am grateful, but doing it
exposed you as a chosen vessel of truth,
a minor prophetess,
a witch with words.
Then you quit.
You held your peace
against a world famished for truth
and needful.
What wonderful stories
danced through your head and
purged your heart but were
left unspoken,
and are now lost?
It's as if you killed the mockingbird
yourself.

Salmon on Toast

I like to make a white sauce by starting with soft butter which I work into flour with a fork to make a paste. Then I add a little milk (or cream when I have it) at a time and when it gets runny I put it on the stove over medium high heat and add more milk and a little salt and lots of pepper and cook it until it's just the way I want it. Today, for lunch, I added a can of salmon to the sauce and poured it over buttered toast and ate it while I watched the executives of WorldCom take the fifth on CNN. No news about Martha. She is probably picking fresh garden peas today, which I often like to put in my white sauce.

Quecreek Mine

I'm eating blueberries and cream
sitting under a ceiling fan
to fight the summer's heat.
And deep in the earth
in Pennsylvania
a trapped miner
taps against
a steel drill stem.
A desperate cadence
Unsteady,
like my heart.

Speed Skating

A coiled spring
of flesh and bones
releasing violently and rewinding instantly
in the most wonderful series of
elegant and awful
explosions.
Razor sharp
steel blades singing
ringing, ripping, cracking
crashing against crystal clear
ice in a constant crazy
cadence of controlled
catastrophe.
Pushing
the limits of
equilibrium, straining in a
super human battle with the powers
of gravity and friction to
produce breakneck
speed.

In a Parallel Universe

In a parallel universe
I walked out into the street
and was struck by a speeding
Good Humor van.
"That was deadly," I observed.
"Why didn't I hear the music?"
I came back into the house
and found yet another universe.
"This seems random," I thought,
"But that's science!"

You could feel the winter wind.

You could feel the
winter wind
in the way the yard
was full of
barren trees like
webs with a few lonely
leaves looking like flies
trapped and desiccated.
All the flesh of summer
gone forever, it seemed,
hopeless
cold,
not just dormant.
Dead.

The Book of Mormon (My Complaint)

Sometimes I beg,
"Don't try to tell me everything
in every phrase," but it's like
a hologram
every fraction contains
all the information of the whole
and who am I to
ask God to take it easy.
After all,
He wrote the book and
dared me to absorb it
promising that if I would
He would give me more.
The truth of all things.
It's in the book.

Tom (being parenthetically parental):
"Okay my little children, time for your dose of anapestic medicine. Hold your noses and open wide.... Wider. Okay, here it comes."

Everyone else (gagging):
"Auughhh!!"

Tom (being parenthetically patronizing):
"There, that wasn't so bad was it? I feel better already."

In this bumpity, bumpity truck that we ride

I am fighting for balance and cling to the side
In this bumpity, bumpity truck that we ride.
I'm surrounded by others who constantly fall
And I'm sure that my fate will be just like them all.
And yet still I fight hard just to keep in the box
As we drive up this road full of potholes and rocks.
And I wonder at times since this trip is no prize
If to struggle so hard is judicious and wise.
Since no one has been able to hold to the top
They all fall, but this truck never comes to a stop.
Something seems to be saying "To fall is no shame,
But it's failing to help other riders brings blame.
And that nothing's as mean or as nasty to friends
As to quit on this journey before your strength ends."
So I strive as I struggle to hold to the rails
To make some sort of diff'rence before my grip fails.
In this bumpity, bumpity truck that we ride
In this bumpity, bumpity truck that we ride.

Be a Lawyer

"Be a lawyer"
he reminded himself
as he swept into the place
Dark suit
White shirt
Silk tie
Shiny black leather shoes with laces and
wearing his careful cunning smile
And trying to keep his mind
prickly and strong.
His lovely lawyer's wife holding on to his arm
so easily that it looked almost voluntary.
"These people won't ever guess that I'm in sales".

I Ask Myself a Question
By Tom "Google" Matkin

I ask myself a question
Does this outfit make me look too young?
I ask myself a question
Could a past life be affecting him now?
I ask myself a question
What is it I am trying to accomplish?
I ask myself a question
Should I shoot? If I shoot my season is over. But, if I don't,
this deer
may be larger next year...
I ask myself a question
How much can you spend?
I ask myself a question
Why do you drive on a parkway and walk on a
walkway?...
I ask myself a question
Why does every Mexican I know want to be a cop?

144

I ask myself a question
How can I convey to this disciple the nature of his
problem?
I ask myself a question
How will this help the folks at home?
I ask myself a question
Is it okay to cheat?
I ask myself a question
WHY DIDN'T I GET VACCINATED?!
I ask myself a question
WHO IS LEONIE?
I ask myself a question
How can I sell myself on employers without having a
college degree?
I ask myself a question
How do white people become allies of black people in
combating racism?
I ask myself a question
How do you sell somebody a record?
I ask myself a question
How can I make myself throw up?
I ask myself a question
How do I know that I am going where I need to go and
doing what I need
to do?
I ask myself a question
What am I passionate about?
I ask myself a question
Who's alive and who's dead?
I ask myself a question
What's the trick to painting your own nails? Whenever I
try to give
myself a manicure, the polish always looks sloppy...
I ask myself a question
Will I be going to LA to do the NBC pilot?
I ask myself a question
Do I hate myself?

I ask myself a question
DID I DO EVERYTHING POSSIBLE TO HELP MY TEAM
BE AS SUCCESSFUL AS
POSSIBLE?
I ask myself a question
How did they do that?
I ask myself a question
What would it be like to be a carp?
I ask myself a question
What is the meaning of life?
I ask myself a question
Why do people question everything?

The Starting Line

This is the starting line
put your toe against the chalk and lean into the future
listen for the starter's pistol
stay loose, stay strong, be ready, be relaxed, be sure
and blast out of the blocks.
Your enemy is time, your enemy is time
and your friend, your only friend, is distance down the
track
get away from that line
scream for your friend, flee from you enemy
it will be over before you know it
it will be over before you know it.

Rolling Coins

We have a two dollar coin in Canada
that we call the Toonie
because, of course, our one dollar coin,
the one with the image of a loon stamped on it,
is called the Loonie
And I can rest five or six Toonies (or Loonies)
stacked together along the bottoms of my fingers
and if I lick my thumb just right
I can roll the Toonie closest to my fingertips
over the stack and place it at the bottom of the stack,
near the palm of my hand,
then reach back with my thumb and roll the next one up
and over the stack and so on and so on and so on.
I learned to do this in France with 50 centime pieces
before Loonie's were even thought of and about that same
time I learned to roll a coin in steady summersaults
across the tops of my fingers, then catching it with my
thumb
as I let it slip between my ring finger and pinky
and then moving it with that same thumb
quickly across the bottom of my hand and starting the
summersaults
over my pointer finger all over again and again and again.
You can do this with Quarters as well,
and with either hand, or with both hands at the same time
if you practice for a bit,
but you can't wear a wedding ring
and roll the coins across your left hand.
I found that out.

How Do You Like Your Eggs?

"How do you like your eggs?" he asked
In his calm existential way
and I wondered what his question meant
Or was it just crafty word play?

"HOW do you like your eggs?" he asked
Over easy or poached or soft....
What is he...? really... A chef! I laughed
Then to cover my smile I coughed.

"How DO you like your eggs?" he asked
With the air of a man in the know
And it made me suspect that he wasn't so nice
But my answer was "Scrambled and slow."

"How do YOU like your eggs?" he asked
As he picked me out of the crowd
My ego was challenged and bruised just a bit
But I thought, "I like eggs that are proud".

"How do you LIKE your eggs?" he asked
As I wiped the yolk off of my chin
"I love 'em, I love 'em, I love 'em, I do!"
So I asked for six more with a grin.

"How do you like YOUR eggs?" he asked
Looking down on my plate with disgust
I was mixing in ketchup and strawberry jam
Til they came out the color of rust.

"How do you like your EGGS?" he asked
As he carefully cut in to his lamb
And he daintily spread on a bit of mint sauce
While I stirred in some mustard and spam.

"How do you like your eggs?" he asked
In his calm existential way
and I wondered what his question meant
Or was it just crafty word play?

Perhaps you've heard...
Another offering by Tom "Google" Matkin

Perhaps you've heard... it's time for a reality check.
Perhaps you've heard...my bathroom sink is quite small.
Perhaps you've heard...the expression "it's darkest just
before dawn." Is
this really true?
Perhaps you've heard...me on the radio, speaking about the
exciting new
option that you, and all Con Edison customers, now have.
Perhaps you've heard... it's high in sugar; perhaps you
could consider
fresh, tinned and dried fruits.
Perhaps you've heard...that they are the same (as I first
did). Let's
clear up some of this confusion.
Perhaps you've heard...that if you love someone, you should
let him/her
go. Go?
Perhaps you've heard...of the A-Team? Ten years ago a
crack commando unit
was sent to prison by a military court for a crime they
didn't commit.
Perhaps you've heard...of me? You probably know me best
...
Perhaps you've heard...of Hydrogen Hydroxide: a colorless,
odorless
liquid; a powerful coolant and solvent; an easily-
synthesized compound
which is used by industry.

149

Perhaps you've heard...of "pass the trash", the tactic of sending a
problem administrator on to other school districts with gleaming
recommendations, so that they don't have to be dealt with anymore.
Perhaps you've heard...the buzz about startup companies recently and
wondered, what exactly is a startup and is it a good place for me to
begin my career?
Perhaps you've heard...of this little organization called The US Marine
Corps?
Perhaps you've heard ... of HDML and you've heard of WML, but you don't
know the differences, and you don't know which to use.
Perhaps you've heard ... of speed dating--the hyper-condensed approach to
courtship that has become a hip way for busy urbanites to meet other
singles.
Perhaps you've heard...you've got cancer. What now?

November Wind

The wind was back again today
an angry, hard wind
and cold
threatening
asking for trouble, fearless
we try to keep low
as we rush for shelter
two handed grabs at car doors
hats in our hands

150

baring our heads
hunching our shoulders
nullifying our necks
and burying our chins in our chests
hugging our collars
wiping our faces of the tears blown out of unwilling eyes
a dirty wind
no one's friend, defying any thanksgiving.

Cheering them on

Not just anyone is allowed
they have to be the best and we make them earn it
prove themselves worthy
then we pay the freight
because they belong to us
and we cheer them
honor them
and off they go
buying into the dream that we have built into them
while we watch stupidly
in shock
at the inevitable
result of what we have done.
Then we praise them
try to cheer their loved ones
and honor them.
While somewhere
on a desk
sits a stack
of applications from
today's dreamers
some of whom will
also go bravely
to their death.

I See You

I see you
standing there proudly defiant
so certain that you are right
not listening to me
not even able to listen
or hear
or feel
or understand what I am saying
because you have judged me
and finding me proud and defiant
and untrustworthy
you will not listen
you cannot listen
and I wonder
as I look at you
standing there
so proud
and so haughty,
Is that really you?
Or am I looking in a mirror?

I Sleep on Live Coals

I sleep on live coals
burning against my back
under the ashes of guilt.
The pain is NOT exquisite
there is no rest
only torment
at least that's
what I think
until I wake up
sweating
gasping
to the realization
that once again
I have fallen asleep
with my electric blanket set on "HI".

Summer Morning

Up at 7:00 a.m. to start
real barbeque and the sprinklers
pull a few weeds and
then cook some eggs.
The smoke from distant
fires clouds my sky
and stings my throat
I read the morning paper
and hope the wind will shift.

Visiting Liberty

I had never been here before
but it seemed familiar to me
as I splashed off the Interstate
and dropped down into the
deep misty ditch that is and was
Liberty.
The rain beat quietly on
my windshield and I drove
without seeing a sign or
reading a map through the
grey afternoon directly to the
Jail.
I circled the block to find where I should park
and I forgot about the rain,
there was no traffic and I parked
alone in the lot without
thinking about anything but
Joseph.
I got out of the car and the rain stopped
I pushed the button in my hand
and the headlights flashed to signal
that it was locked and I remembered
that just 24 hours before I had been in
Carthage.
Actually, every few hours it had been the same
another empty parking lot, more rain,
and the obligatory tour and interrogation
by another earnest missionary couple
and me, distracted, distant, cool, in my own
Prison.
I had been left alone for a time
in that cell/bedroom where it actually happened
and I had sat, very still, in the window,
looking down through the rain streaked glass
running section 135 through my mind, word for

Word.
After Liberty I would go to Independence
where I wouldn't even get out of the car
because I needed to get to Adam-Ondi-Ahman before dark
where I would drive around the loop on a shiny wet road
knowing that tomorrow I would see the
Sun.

Got it Done

The air was so thick with rancor
that words seemed to pass through
it in super slo-mo and yet the
home teachers seemed determined
not to notice
delivering the prescribed
monthly message
about being kind
to widows)
by reading carelessly
selected passages
then offering the
obligatory generic word of prayer
before scurrying back into
the night so that the combatants could
resume their losing battle.

Saturday's Work

I should have been in the garden today
turning the tired earth in the cold wind
with a long handled shovel preparing it
for another winter season
but early on the thought came to visit the temple
and instead of leaving after just one
session, as I had planned, I stayed for
three, saving John, Sigurden, and Albino
from out of their long winter season
and easing my own pain.

This Riddle

This riddle now is one I poses
Of when to poke next door our noses
To ask a vase for red red roses
Or borrow salt, or other choses,*
One time we had to share imposes
But now the Stuff-Mart never closes!

* Latin-legal term for "things" pronounced "shoses"

The Winter after he Died

When she walked around the lake
usually in the early morning,
she had taken to looking ahead
and if that certain fence post
looked like it had an extra foot
of misshapen height to it,
she would skirt off the pathway
and stay clear of her new friend
the eagle jealously
surveying his territory.
It was a small lake
a large pond really
but the walk was along rough ground
and was far enough to invigorate
and exercise her heart.
Among the ice huts
sometimes a solitary figure or two
would be sitting on a plastic bucket
hunched over a fishing hole
in studied isolation
and no one ever took any note of her.
She often saw a fox
and just as often deer
and always birds
pelicans in the open water
and ducks and geese
stopping by on their migrations.
One morning, as she left her quiet house
she was startled by a huge owl
like a visiting royal
sitting in state
on the lowest branch of her giant cottonwood
in the front yard not far from her kitchen window.
Her plans to walk vanished
as she made herself small

and circled the tree from a distance
never taking her eyes off of the visitor
and ending up back in the house standing by the sink
staring out the window
drawing her breath as quietly as possible
willing it to stay
to feel welcome, connected,
at home.
The furnace fan growled to life
sounding like thunder to her
and she looked down to see
she was standing in a puddle of water
which had been snow on her boots.
When she looked up again
the owl was gone.

This fumbling testing time

This fumbling testing time
learning to be a god
like a mewling babe is
learning to play a
Bach Fugue or a Mozart Minuet
and yet Bach is there to
be heard by the babe
and the keyboard is there
to be slobbered upon and
pounded by tiny fists
beating on the very notes
that could be turned into
rolling fugues and singing
minuets.

And so, for now, we
are babes, all awkward, crude
hoping to amuse and please
and barely glimpsing the exquisiteness
of things both small and great.

Into the School of Plenty

Into the school of plenty
a father and child
came
and the father left
but the child did not
come to class
and so his teacher
sought him out
and finding the lad
sobbing
in a corner
asked,
"are you hurt?"
thinking the father may
have been rough with his son
but the boy choked out
"no"
and so the teacher asked
"are you sick?"
still crying the boy nodded
"no"
"then whatever is the matter?"
asked the teacher tenderly
and the boy, composed himself
for a second with great difficulty
and gasped:
"I'm hungry!"

After Seminary Grad

The twins ran together across the lawn
hand in hand
hearts knit
gowns flowing
identical
sparkling blue flowers
against the solid green and shining granite
painting the temple grass
celebrating the freedom that only a young graduate can
know
dancing
all a caper
giddy and sad at the same time
but always,
always
one.

Pictures on the Funeral Home Wall

Her lips were too too full
her hair too curly
and far too red
and she was beyond young
she was new
hopeful
faithful
fresh
courageous
and immortal
in the large portrait
surrounded by two dozen snapshots of her life
There were a couple
with her handsome young husband
ready for war

A few more with him
as he and she grew out of their uniforms
and played, worked, worried, succeeded and celebrated and
wearied together
Lots with her children
and grandchildren
A few with friends
One where she
tended to him as he sat in his wheelchair
And several more where
his image was
conspicuously absent.
A lifetime spent,
well spent,
and worthy
of celebration
of remembrance
of love.

Why You Can't Go Home Again

You can't go home again
because the house you once lived in has shrunk.
You can't go home again
because the front porch, once
scene to long distance tricycle races with
your brother
now would not store a single adult sized bicycle and
you would have to stoop to cross it in a single step.
You can't go home again
because the basement that once opened
to the driveway and
where day long swash buckling sword battles
multi game hockey tournaments
hide and seek wars played with nineteen cousins
and the all the boys from two blocks

and massive month long clean up projects prevailed
is now practically only a crawl space
with a brief opening to the world
too steep, too creepy, too cold
too dark and too low
to even think of passing through.
You can't go home again
because the yard
once a lush, diverse and rich ecosystem
stretching into two time zones
with sink holes, mines, caverns, plains, forests
mountains, deserts, golf courses,
coliseums, two baseball diamonds
an abandoned airport and vast
gardens and spacious lawns
where countless nations of cowboys and Indians
perished and dreams of athletic
geophysical and geopolitical conquest were born
and died as well is now a tiny speck of lawn
with a tired looking tree in
the middle
You can't go home again
because the driveway, once
a freeway, country lane, graveled road
and playground that took
three boys and a father in
his suit and tie a month to
shovel off after every winter snow storm
is now barely big enough to park a single
car, which covers it so well no snow
could possibly accumulate around it.
You can't go home again
because the kitchen where
your big sisters, your mom, your
5 aunts and your grandmother
and 22 women from the neigbourhood
could all gather to bottle peaches,

cherries, raspberries, and pears
and to put up the harvest of corn, beans
and beets from the acres of
gardens out back
where ovens, walk in coolers and freezers
battalions of sinks, miles of
counters and cupboards
held a vast and mysterious
array of culinary
tools and stores and where
these matrons of mercy
and providence and mirth
would relax while waiting for
bread to rise and pies to bake
by picking away
at the 3 quilts set up in frames in the far corners of
the room
which is now filled
with a single small table
pushed up against the only window
so one person at a time
might get by to tend
the stove and clean
the dishes in the single
sink beside the tiny fridge.
You can't go home again because
your upstairs bedroom
once a magnificent hall, spacious dormatory
and playroom all together, sleeping any number
and easily allowing games of tackle
football, basketball, and soccer
at once
with a makeshift tent village
made for the babies from blankets and chairs
in one corner and where
boys played marbles on the
scrap of carpet in anther

and girls marshaled legions of dolls and
truckloads of costumes for dress up
in yet another and where a double glass door opened
to a balcony on the roof
where nine more could sleep
in uncommon comfort under the stars
is now a spare and cold
cell with only a tiny
bed and one window
too high to see out of
too low to crawl through
too narrow to open
and too small to find.
You can't go home again
because the living room
where everyone you once
knew would gather for
the holidays and for birthdays
and for missionary farewells
and homecomings
and where the uncles
on your mom's side would
talk politics and laugh and
argue for days and where
the uncles on your
dad's side would sit
awkwardly and say nothing
for hours
and where your grandmother
would sit and knit long into the night
and sometimes would
share a story about
her youth or her widowhood
or where you would
just tell her about your
hurt feelings or your big game
or your small day

You can't go home again
You can't go home again
because
that living room
that place of prayer
and peace and argument
and books and visitors
and music, noisy games
rough and gentle play
grief and joy
friends and family
occasional strangers
and love
because that place
that beating heart
of the family
that central station of the grand
journey of your life
that generation of good
that hospital
that resort
that refuge
that chapel
theatre
library
school
and
temple
is now
still.

Reflections on D&C 18:10

Please get along with each other
my children
souls of men and boys,
women and girls
be gentle, be wise, be sweet
be tenderhearted you benefactors
of the constant tender mercies of your Maker
Be forgiving, swift to forget offences, slow to forget any
kindness
Remember the worth
of that soul
and your own
bought and paid for in terrible sacrifice
Worth that your fierce countenance seeks to deny
Sacrifice that your disregard rejects
but which God has proclaimed
value irrefutable and immutable
true and forever.

Please get along with each other
my children.

My Hands

Hands with minds of their own
Independent of my distracted state
They carry on with my daily life
Molding, twisting, tying, pulling
Grabbing, rubbing, poking
Holding, stroking, pinching
(love those opposable thumbs)
Self motivated, skilled servants
Quick learners and steady companions
Seldom do they ask for directions from me.

Shopping at Costco

I push my cart through Costco and
see the many infants masked as
mature adults doing the same thing.
I see through them
because I'm one of them
We have aged together
and I know the secret
that being a grandparent is
just talk to conceal the truth
that we haven't really
changed, we are still young
fresh, naïve, raw and prattling
Babes. Not just young but
juvenile at heart. Parading around
in our aged disguises.
We fill our carts with things we
didn't know we needed until we
saw them on the shelves.
We have gray hair now, and are
labored in our pursuit of happiness
bent over, sore, heavy, slow
shopping to find hope
knowing the cost of everything
and the value of nothing.
It would be pathetic, but the lie
is so well kept, so well guarded
that we believe it.
Which, of course,
just makes it that much
more pitiable
as we line
up to
cash out
leaning heavily on our
overburdened carts.

Riding Above the River

The river cuts the prairie like a butcher with his knife
Exposing and disposing of the evidence of life
And up above the valley where the range seems safely whole
I ride a wild pony without any real control.

He gallops to the precipice between the floor and sky
Then turns, unbid, and races for the fence beyond my eye
Each turn a little closer to disaster and despair
Each trip a little faster and each grasp is graced with prayer.

The river's razor reaches out and every rider knows
That he will someday have to follow where the river flows
I fight the terror of the ride and try to find the reins
And guide my horse towards the hope of unseen higher plains.

We're both unruly, proud I guess, and will not yield our wills
And so my life's uncertain as it's played out on these hills.

What rhymes with blood?

I want a word that rhymes with blood.
I might use flood or flower bud
Or make a line that ends in mud
But I despair of using dud
Or crud or spud or scud or cud
Or stud or thud or hud or rudd,
When I require a rhyme for blood.

Too tired to count

How many medals won today?
How many drunks in jail?
How many lost in city streets?
How many hearts gone stale?

How many lightning strikes tonight?
How many dancing slow?
How many reaching for the stars?
How many stuck in snow?

How many still in bed at noon?
How many die too young?
How many twisting in the wind?
How many songs unsung?

How many breathing far too hard?
How many chances missed?
How many cliches in this poem?
How many? Make a list!

I'd like to add the numbers up
To see the true amount
But dawn is not too far away
And I'm too tired to count.

When you joined this church

When you joined this church
did anyone mention that you
would become a citizen
of the City of Nauvoo
at the same time
and that pioneer
blood would begin
to run in your veins
and that the prophet
would become
your prophet
and the bishop
your bishop
did they tell you
your name too would
become known
for good and for evil
throughout the world
and that you would
long to visit Utah
now and then
and stand in the
shadow of that
temple
and those
everlasting
hills
and that
our burdens
our pain our joy
and our
story
would
become
your

burden
your pain
your joy
and your story
if you stayed
faithful?

Made in the USA
Charleston, SC
29 October 2011